BEYOND NEOLIBERALISM, NATIONALISM AND SOCIALISM

About the Centre for Progressive Capitalism

The Centre for Progressive Capitalism's mission is to develop policies and influence policymakers to instigate a more progressive and democratic capitalism. We are hosted by Policy Network, a leading international thinktank promoting the best progressive thinking on major social and economic challenges. Our work is led by a cross-party advisory board and a steering group of technical and policy experts. We undertake original research and promote debate through publications, expert seminars and public engagement.

www.progressive-capitalism.net

BEYOND NEOLIBERALISM, NATIONALISM AND SOCIALISM

Rethinking the boundary between state and market

Edited by
Thomas Aubrey

Centre for
Progressive
Capitalism

ROWMAN & LITTLEFIELD
INTERNATIONAL

London • New York

Published by Rowman & Littlefield International Ltd
Unit A, Whitacre, 26-34 Stannary Street, London, SE11 4AB
www.rowmaninternational.com

Rowman & Littlefield International Ltd. is an affiliate of Rowman & Littlefield
4501 Forbes Boulevard, Suite 200, Lanham, Maryland 20706, USA
With additional offices in Boulder, New York, Toronto (Canada), and Plymouth (UK)
www.rowman.com

British Library Cataloguing in Publication Data

A catalogue record for this book is available from the British Library

ISBN: PB 978-1-78660-477-4
ISBN: eBook 978-1-78660-478-1

Library of Congress Cataloging-in-Publication Data
Library of Congress Control Number: 2017941125

♾™ The paper used in this publication meets the minimum requirements of
American National Standard for Information Sciences—Permanence of Paper for
Printed Library Materials, ANSI/NISO Z39.48-1992.

Printed in the United States of America

CONTENTS

ABOUT THE CONTRIBUTORS

Thomas Aubrey

Thomas Aubrey is director of the Centre for Progressive Capitalism and founder of Credit Capital Advisory.

Kate Barker

Kate Barker is an economist who served previously as a member of the Bank of England's Monetary Policy Committee. She has advised the British government on social issues, such as housing and health care, and is a senior visiting fellow in the Department of Land Economy at the University of Cambridge.

Sharon Bowles

Sharon Bowles is a Liberal Democrat member of the House of Lords and served as a member of the European parliament for south east England from 2005 to 2014. She was chair of the European parliament's Economic and Monetary Affairs Committee. She is a non-executive director of the London Stock Exchange and a member of the Systemic Risk Council.

Vince Cable

Vince Cable served as secretary of state for business, innovation and skills between 2010 and 2015. He was the Liberal Democrat member of parliament for Twickenham for 18 years and served as deputy leader of the Liberal Democrats.

Andrew Cooper

Andrew Cooper is a Conservative member of the House of Lords and the co-founder of the research and strategy consultancy Populus. He was the prime minister's director of strategy between 2011 and 2013.

Patrick Diamond

Patrick Diamond is co-chair of Policy Network and a lecturer in Public Policy at Queen Mary, University of London, Gwilym Gibbon fellow at Nuffield College, Oxford, and a visiting fellow in the Department of Politics at the University of Oxford. Previously, he was head of policy planning in 10 Downing Street and senior policy adviser to the prime minister.

Andrew Gamble

Andrew Gamble is professor of Politics at the University of Sheffield and emeritus professor of Politics at the University of Cambridge. His most recent book is *Crisis Without End? The Unravelling of Western Prosperity*.

Stephen Green

Stephen Green is a Conservative member of the House of Lords and was minister for trade and investment between 2011 and 2013. He was previously group chief executive and group chairman of HSBC Group.

Lawrence Hamilton

Lawrence Hamilton is the NRF/British Academy Research Chair in Political Theory, Department of Political Studies, University of the Witwatersrand and the Department of Politics and International Studies (POLIS), University of Cambridge. He is editor-in-chief of *Theoria: A Journal of Social and Political Theory*.

Stephen Kinnock

Stephen Kinnock is Labour member of parliament for Aberavon. Prior to his parliamentary career, Stephen held positions at the British Council and the World Economic Forum.

Dina Medland

Dina Medland is an independent writer, editor and commentator focused on corporate governance, ethics and the workings of the boardroom. She has been a contributor to Forbes Europe and formerly worked at the Financial Times.

John Plender

John Plender is a columnist at the Financial Times specialising in economic and monetary policy. His most recent book is *Capitalism: Money, Morals and Markets*. He has served as chair of the Pensions and Investment Research Consultants (PIRC) and a FTSE 350 company.

Alastair Reed

Alastair Reed is a consumer policy analyst. Previously he was a senior policy researcher at Policy Network and the Centre for Progressive Capitalism.

David Sainsbury

David Sainsbury was minister for science and innovation between 1998 and 2006 and has been the chancellor of the University of Cambridge since 2011.

Jenny Tooth

Jenny Tooth is the chief executive of the UK Business Angels Association. She has over 20 years' experience supporting SMEs to access investment, both in the UK and internationally.

BEYOND NEOLIBERALISM, NATIONALISM AND SOCIALISM

Reflections on the ideological vacuum of our age

Thomas Aubrey

Since the fall of the Berlin Wall in 1989 there has been a tendency by political commentators to describe events as 'historic'. Such everyday use is largely unhelpful given that most reported events will not turn out to have much significance at all in the way we live our lives. The challenge of course is that it may take decades to fully understand which ones are significant and deserving of the label historic.

To what extent 2016 will change the way western democracies run themselves, in the words of Zhou Enlai, "it is too early to say". It may well turn out to be an inflexion point signalling the end of the neoliberal economic system that has dominated Anglo-Saxon political economy since the early 1980s. This broad doctrine, which promoted lower taxes and public expenditure, freer labour and product markets and privatisation in conjunction with support for globalisation, was expected to create a prosperous society for all. In 2016, voters in western democracies decided otherwise. However, one should not assume that this shift by the electorate necessarily signals the end of neoliberalism.

When an ideology is considered to have outlived its usefulness to society, it has generally been replaced with a new set of ideas, which have been steadily galvanising support in the wings. However, the two most coherent set of ideas that are currently on offer to electorates and which are opposed to neoliberalism actually precede its development: democratic socialism and populism based along national lines. During the 1930s when liberalism last came under attack, both of these ideologies offered hope to the disaffected in society. However, neither option turned out particularly well for humanity, as the 20th century demonstrated.

The clamour for change from both camps to move away from a society grounded in neoliberal principles has been to advocate a far greater role for the state. However, beyond pulling out of free trade discussions and the promotion of the nationalisation of the railways, comparisons to the interwar era are greatly exaggerated. Indeed, it remains to be seen whether the death knell has actually been sounded for the neoliberal system at all.

Given that the initial rise of the neoliberal consensus was formed partly due to a perceived failure of big government, it is feasible that both movements will largely keep the existing neoliberal system in place and instead tinker around the edges with policies aimed at core supporters. However, if electorates do not see these policies as having sufficient impact, then a more extreme politics may well arise at some point in the future.

One key question for western democracies is therefore whether there might be another way to reform our economic system to drive inclusive growth without having to return to the failed ideologies of the 20th century. It is this question that this publication seeks to explore in some depth. A politics that believes in harnessing the dynamic power of markets, but also one that recognises that markets fail more frequently than some would like us to believe. A politics that doesn't believe the state can be an all-powerful and knowing entity, but a state that can still be active to improve the lives of its citizens.

Gandhi once said that the future depends on what you do today. Voters have made it clear they are unhappy with the current economic system, but it is less clear what they would prefer to have in its place. Although the role of government is to prioritise the welfare of the inhabitants of a country, how this is achieved matters. If western democracies are unable to improve their current economic system, they may well find themselves staring into the abyss of domestic and international upheaval once more.

However, reform is difficult and can be a hard sell to voters, which is why politicians appear to be taking a more populist approach to address electoral concerns. The challenge is that simple theories such as populism, socialism or neoliberalism ignore the complexity of our economy and society. As such, a more pragmatic approach to politics that focuses once more on the common good of society may well be a more fruitful place to start rethinking a political economy that can work for everyone.

This publication is divided into four parts. The first section assesses the breakdown in legitimacy of the current neoliberal consensus. The essays explore voters' increasing disillusionment with neoliberalism, and worries about unconstrained immigration and the politics of identity – factors that were clearly present during the various political campaigns of 2016.

The essays in the second section explore how a progressive political economy needs to embrace the market, but with an enabling state to manage its downside risks. It is noted that the failure of neoliberalism to create a framework for inclusive growth is partly related to its utilitarian underpinning, which ignores the needs of individuals in society. Such reflections are not dissimilar to those posed by JM Keynes during the interwar years, as faith in the liberal order began to wane.

The third section develops practical policy ideas to resolve key systemic market failures that have acted as major barriers to inclusive growth. The essays elaborate on the persistent lack of access to housing, to equity capital for scale-ups and to technical skills education. Increasing the availability of these factors of production is central to the success of a progressive capitalism.

The final section turns to the behaviour of the corporate sector, which emphasises that the gap between the expectations of society and the conduct of business must begin to narrow. The essays highlight that firms have become increasingly divorced from the common good of society, which has reflected itself in numerous ways, including rocketing executive pay and a crisis in pensions with record underfunding of pension liabilities.

Such a rethink of our political economy is critical if society is to rebuild its faith in public and private sector institutions, and to prevent extremism emerging once more.

A DISENCHANTED ELECTORATE

BEYOND IMMIGRATION

The search for policy responses to the populist surge must look to infrastructure and education

Andrew Cooper

The year of 2016 will forever be associated with the populist surges that ambushed the political establishment, taking Britain out of the European Union and installing Donald Trump in the White House.

In Trump's encapsulation, it was a vote 'for nationalism and against globalism'. Emotive and often bitterly divisive debate revealed a deep gulf in both countries between, as Tony Blair put it, 'open' and 'closed' outlooks. Those who believe in globalism – and that an open economy is innately better than a closed one – need to reflect frankly on how and why these arguments were lost in 2016, or they will continue to lose.

Polling failed to foresee the victories for Brexit and Trump, but deep data analysis of the results tells us a great deal about the forces driving the march of populism. This starts with the important conclusion that the demographic pattern of leave voters in the UK and Trump voters in the US was almost identical. The significance of this is further underlined by the fact that the same pattern also applied to voters in the Austrian presidential election for the narrowly defeated ultra-nationalist Norbert Hofer, those in Italy who voted successfully to reject Matteo Renzi's constitutional reforms, and the supporters of the Front National in France who are lining up enthusiastically behind the 2017 presidential election campaign of Marine Le Pen. The same forces, more or less, are changing the political landscape in these countries and others; they charged the campaigns of Geert Wilders in the Dutch election in March and will charge those of the Alternative für Deutschland party in Germany's election in the autumn.

There is no single demographic factor behind these political movements and a lot of commentary has over-simplified what happened, often in order to confirm pre-existing biases about the right political response. On the left, many have wanted to believe that the political eruptions of 2016 were, in essence, the revolt of the economically left-behind against a failing global economic orthodoxy – caused by inequality. On the right, many have preferred to conclude that these votes were the assertion of national identity and economic self-interest over a metropolitan elite internationalist consensus.

Close examination of micro-level demographics reveals a rather more nuanced picture. There is a stark geographical pattern in the support for Brexit, Trump, Hofer and Le Pen, as well as a consistent demographic pattern. Archetypally, support was anchored among voters who shared not one or two demographic factors in common, but several. Compared to the average in their country, they were older, whiter, less well-educated, living on lower incomes and in lower-value housing; they were more likely to be obese and in less than good health. Definitively these voters were concentrated in places characterised by lack of diversity; homogeneous areas of ever more heterogeneous countries. Voting behaviour was strongly driven by people's proximity to diversity as well as by their social and economic situation; to make sense of what happened we must take account of both of these dimensions.

The 2016 US election map shows that poorer rural areas voted predominantly for Trump. But analysis at the level of the 3,143 US counties rather than its 50 states, reveals a more pixelated map in which the most unequal areas of America swung away from the Republicans, not towards them; income inequality is, overall, negatively correlated with support for Trump. Over the last 10 presidential elections, the average Democrat voter has become steadily wealthier and the average Republican voter steadily poorer – but over the same period cultural and identity politics have grown in impact too: the diversity dimension has become increasingly significant. Trump's victory came from a coalition of relatively prosperous, predominantly white traditionally Republican voters and relatively poor, overwhelmingly white former Democrat voters.

Brexit, like Trump, did best in less urban, more rural areas – and in places where the population has been getting older; support for the UK staying in the EU, like support for Hillary Clinton, was much stronger in urban, especially metropolitan areas, and in places where the population has been getting younger. Over recent years, more economically and socially mobile people (who tend also to be younger) have moved into more urban and diverse places; the places they have moved *from* have become correspondingly older and 'left behind' physically and culturally as much as economically.

Cultural attitude was a strong determinant of how people voted in both the EU referendum and the US election – much more so than party affinity or economic situation alone. There is, for example, a close and direct correlation between whether someone voted remain/ Clinton or leave/Trump and their feelings about concepts like multiculturalism, globalisation, social liberalism, the Green movement and feminism. Those who view these things as a force for good were overwhelmingly likely, if they are British, to support staying in the EU and, if they are American, to support Hillary Clinton.

This tells us something important: for most who voted in the momentous electoral tests of 2016 – in Italy and Austria as well as the US and Britain – the decision was the consequence of a worldview, not just a pragmatic judgement about a political choice. This helps to explain why leave voters in Britain were utterly unmoved – perhaps even further emboldened – by the imperative warnings of the mainstream establishment and the 'experts'. It helps to explain why Trump voters in the US discounted arguments that he was not a fit person to be president.

The theme, perhaps, is 'disconnection', which has a broader connotation than 'left-behind'. Two tribes of voters disconnected from one another's life experience, cultural touchstones and worldview. One group of voters feeling disconnected from the direction in which their country seems to be going. The same group of voters disconnected from the opportunities that seem, increasingly, confined to large towns and cities. In Britain this also translates into a deep and growing antipathy, in the rest of the country, towards London, from which the disconnection feels most profound.

London – easily the most diverse part of the UK – voted 60:40 to remain in the EU. Many Londoners view the city as an open, cosmopolitan hub. To many others, London seems more like an island of prosperity that is open to the rest of the world, but closed to the rest of Britain. London – and other big towns and cities – have a proximity to opportunity, information, skills and networks; they are connected, not disconnected.

The political debate since the EU referendum, especially among those who unsuccessfully campaigned for a remain vote, has focused on immigration (or 'free movement') more than any other single issue. For many of those who voted leave, by far the biggest benefit of Brexit was felt to be regaining the power to curb immigration from other EU countries – with all the benefits that they thought that this would bring for Britain: more jobs, shorter NHS waiting times, smaller class sizes, easier access to social housing.

This was the staunch view in Tory heartlands like Lincolnshire, Kent and Essex, just as in Labour bedrocks in Hull, Stoke and Doncaster – all places where more than 70% voted leave. There is an easy logic to the conclusion, which many politicians seem to have reached, that reconnecting with these voters requires mainstream politicians to reverse themselves on immigration, to echo voter concerns about the free movement of labour and to put forward policies, in some form or other, to restrict it.

The demographic analysis of the Brexit vote provides an important reality check to this train of thought. There are parts of Britain that voted heavily to leave the EU and that have been profoundly affected by economic migration from Europe. But they are a minority. Demographic analysis unambiguously shows that the core leave vote was anchored in places that are specifically defined by their lack of diversity; places, in other words, with few, if any, migrants from the EU. This is important for a simple, obvious reason: curbing EU migration would make no material difference to the real problems experienced by people living in these places or the disconnectedness that defines them.

Brighton is a southern seaside town about 70 miles from London, accessible by train in around an hour, for less than £100 per week. More than a fifth of its population was born outside the UK and just under 90% are white, about the same as the national average. Around 16% of the population is aged over 65, similar to the national average, and about 40% are in full-time employment. In the EU referendum Brighton backed staying in the EU by a margin of 69% to 31% – one of the highest remain votes in the country.

Margate is also a southern seaside town about 70 miles from London. It takes at least 90 minutes to get there by train from the capital – and a weekly season ticket costs about £150. Less than 5% of its population was born outside the UK and less than 3% are non-white, while 20% are aged over 65, and only a third are in full-time employment. In the EU referendum Margate voters backed leaving the EU by about a 2:1 margin.

Curbing immigration – if that is indeed the consequence of the UK eventually leaving the EU – will do little or nothing to lift the fortunes of the people of Margate. Even if the net effect of leaving the EU and curbing immigration from EU countries is, eventually, to strengthen Britain's economy – which is far from certain – the benefits are very unlikely to cascade down to the people of Margate, because it won't address the facets of disconnectedness that afflict their town.

The people who lose, even if the country as a whole is slightly better off in the end, will be the people who have been losing for years: those with no skills, old skills or wrong skills; the disconnected. The future holds further great challenges for them; if we map the places where local jobs are most vulnerable to the march of robotics and artificial intelligence, it is by and large the same disconnected places that voted in large numbers for Brexit (and for Trump in the US). Those looming economic pressures cannot be wished away any more than the economic pressures of globalisation could be held at bay or reversed by voting to leave the EU or for President Trump.

Politicians in the political mainstream will no doubt continue to contort themselves in search of a form of words on immigration that will reconnect them with voters and, they hope, win them permission to be heard again on other issues. But this is somewhat to miss the point. Immigration wasn't, ultimately, the driver of the populist uprisings of 2016. Telling voters what they want to hear on immigration skirts around the real problems that are all too readily blamed on immigration, but which curbing immigration won't resolve. The search for policy responses and political solutions needs to look far beyond immigration – to transport, housing, education and retraining, as well as to innovative ways to regenerate the places that have become disconnected.

TIME TO CONCEDE ON FREE MOVEMENT?

Examining the reality of free movement of workers

Vince Cable

All my instincts about immigration are liberal. I enjoy diversity and diverse London in particular. I value having colleagues, friends and family from different national, ethnic and cultural backgrounds (and had a long, successful interracial marriage of my own). I have been in the political trenches fighting racism and anti-immigrant prejudice for half a century, from Enoch Powell's "rivers of blood" to Nigel Farage's army of unwelcome refugees. I am a fully paid up remainer – and remoaner – and did my bit trying to persuade elderly villagers in the prosperous south that 80 million Turks were not about to descend on them. As an economist, I am an old-fashioned and shameless free trader. And I spent five years as secretary of state in the coalition government fighting endless skirmishes with Theresa May's Home Office over the Tory net immigration target and damaging curbs on overseas students and workers.

So I should be out there championing European 'free movement of labour'. But I am not. And I am puzzled by the passionate support of the Corbynite left and many liberals for this particular component of the European single market. There are arguments for and against giving Poles, Romanians and Bulgarians the right to compete in the UK labour market on the same basis as the locals, but I struggle to see what great principle of socialism or liberalism is at stake. Nor do I see why a broadly liberal approach to immigration necessitates unrestricted immigration and unrestricted immigration from some countries but not others.

The reality is that Britain does not offer free movement to foreign workers. Indians, Jamaicans, Australians or Americans who wish to work here – and many of them could enrich the UK economy by doing so – have to pass through a complex, bureaucratic maze of visa restrictions. Their employers have to demonstrate that someone with comparable qualifications is not available within the European Economic Area.

These restrictions are real and severe and, as a local MP, I encountered many instances of their harsh and inflexible application. And for relatives who wish to visit, let alone stay, and for prospective marriage partners, the barriers can be prohibitive. Very little of the coverage of the referendum touched on the uncomfortable fact of the large Brexit vote among Asian ethnic minorities, almost certainly due to resentment at the relatively favourable immigration treatment of eastern Europeans with little historical connection to Britain. They could see clearly, even what liberals and socialists could not, that European 'free movement of labour' was essentially, if not explicitly, for white people.

Once that pretence is stripped away, the argument is about the merits of immigration per se. Indeed there is something rather encouraging about the colour-blind prejudices of British people who were equally affronted by blond people talking in Slavic languages on buses as by brown-skinned people wearing Islamic dress (indeed, surveys suggested that the greatest opposition is to immigrants from Poland and Pakistan to roughly the same degree. Indian nationals, who currently account for almost 60 per cent of all skilled worker visas, appear to attract very little opposition.) Previous immigration 'debates' over Caribbean immigration, then east African and wider Asian immigration, occurred at a time of substantial net emigration. Although the 'debate' was conducted in terms of 'immigration', there were net outflows for most years until the end of the 1980s and the real issue was race: white people leaving and brown and black people entering. This century however the influx has been boosted by eastern Europeans and net immigration has been over 200,000 a year, rising to over 300,000 in 2015 and 2016.

Now the debate is largely about the level of immigration, not race.

THE ECONOMICS

Is unrestricted immigration – albeit from some countries – good for Britain? The economics is broadly supportive of immigration, but not without important qualifications. First, immigrant workers add to national income, but not necessarily income per head. They help to create a bigger economy, but not necessarily a richer one. That will only occur if they are more productive than the average British worker. They are likely to be since they are more mobile, are attracted by particular skill or job market shortages and, almost by definition, are enterprising and ambitious to better themselves. But, as they settle with their families, those benefits are eroded.

Second, immigrants are relatively young, which explains why their contribution to the public realm is likely to be disproportionately positive. They pay more in tax than they take out in benefits or use of the NHS and other public services (except, perhaps, schools). But young people get older and these benefits are non-recurring and become negative in due course. Angela Merkel made use of demographic arguments in justifying her approach to Syrian refugees, but as her critics pointed out, these are temporary benefits, even if real.

Third, the counter-argument from critics of immigration is that immigrants depress wages and reduce job opportunities for natives. This will only be true where immigrants are competing rather than complementary. The fruit pickers of Lincolnshire and East Anglia, the computer whizz-kids of Shoreditch, the medical practitioners, the academic specialists and scientists are hardly competing and may actually create local employment in some instances. But there is more direct competition in building trades, taxi driving and in production line work. When secretary of state, I commissioned a range of academic studies of these impacts. The results were sufficiently reassuring that the Home Office would not allow my department to publish them! There appeared, however, to be some negative impact on wages in recession conditions and there may be problems for particular occupations and locations.

Fourth, there are externalities: spillover effects. Some of these effects are the source of some of the negative feeling about immigration: for instance, allegations that educational and health provision, already under pressure, is made more difficult to access for long-standing residents. For reasons given above, this is unlikely to be an issue in aggregate because the profile of immigrants is more likely to make them net contributors; but it may well be an issue locally, especially when migrant workers bring dependents and become permanent residents.

The most obvious of these negative impacts is in aggravating pressure on housing, especially as migrants tend to gravitate to places where there is employment rather than spare capacity in the housing market. Growing numbers will, other things being equal, push up property prices and rents. The distributional effects are, however, complex; among the beneficiaries will be existing property owners in the areas concerned (some of whom may well be complaining that 'immigrants drive down property prices' when the likelihood is the opposite). Moreover, these impacts are most extreme in urban conurbations like London, which attract most immigrants, but whose pre-existing residents appear more relaxed about the impact than those who are distant. This takes us to the awkward politics of immigration.

THE POLITICS

Surveys of public opinion tend to show that immigration is at or close to the top of issues that concern the public and has been for some years. The only other issue of comparable salience is the state of the economy. The trend in net migration in recent years, currently at record levels, suggests that public concern is rational and based on fact even if there are many particular fears and arguments that are irrational and based on falsehoods or exaggeration.

The specific argument about numbers relates to the government's immigration target originally set out on the 2010 Conservative manifesto (but not endorsed by the coalition) and reiterated in the 2015 manifesto to reduce net migration to under 100,000. As we have seen, net migration increased to over three times that level. The repeated, well advertised, failure to meet the target has been a major contributory factor to the sense that 'immigration is out of control' and to the success of a Brexit campaign built substantially around that theme.

Yet the political damage was in part self-inflicted and related to the very questionable way in which the figures are compiled. The migration figures are arrived at by aggregating several different types of population flows: work related (which include non-EU visas and EU non-visa cases); overseas students; family dependents; asylum seekers and a few small categories as with entrepreneurs. Yet these are quite different in their legal and economic basis and give a quite misleading impression of the scale and nature of immigration.

The most obvious anomaly is the inclusion of overseas students, which were estimated to contribute over 200,000 in 2010-11, though this has declined to around 170,000 a year. In the first three years of the coalition, overseas students outnumbered overseas workers and were the main focus of tougher 'immigration' control. Yet arguably overseas students are not immigrants at all, though they meet the UN definition by coming for over a year (other than those on short courses). They overwhelmingly return home. And while they are here they contribute very positively to the economy by paying full fees (if they are from outside the EU), cross-subsidising British students and spending on local goods and services like tourists. Surveys of public opinion suggest that the public do not see overseas students as part of the 'immigration problem' and regard them positively in general.

The Home Office insists that many stay behind – often illegally – to work, though this is vigorously disputed by others in government, like my former department (Business, Innovation and Skills). The argument hinges around the accuracy of the Home Office 'Passenger Survey'; a far superior method would have been exit checks, which the Home Office declined to pursue because of manpower savings until very recently (the most recent data suggests that the Home Office greatly exaggerated the student over-stayer problem). Removal of students from the immigration numbers would greatly improve the accuracy of the figures and reduce the scale of the problem. It would also reduce the temptation to axe student visas as a quick, if self-defeating, way to make the numbers look 'better'.

Where public perceptions and the numbers tell the same story is in relation to work related migration from eastern Europe. There was an overall rise in work related immigration to over 300,000 (gross) in 2015 and 2016 from 175,000 in 2012 and 62% of the latest figure are from the EU and about 55% of these had a job to go to. Separate figures on national insurance number registration show that there was a surge of around 300,000 between the end of 2013 and March 2015 for EU nationals, while those for non-EU nationals were roughly stable. By far the largest numbers of registrations have been of Romanians and Polish nationality.

The politics of immigration is further complicated by the emotion – positive and negative – around asylum seekers. To put this in perspective, however, there were 44,000 asylum claims in the year to mid 2015 and 11,600 were granted asylum: only around 4% of net immigration.

The central dilemma which appears to have shaped the course the UK government has ended up taking in the Brexit process, is the central requirement in the negotiation to establish some limitation on EU flows, but this runs counter to the requirement of freedom of movement within the EU single market. Had the government not abandoned an ambition to stay in the single market, common sense suggests that it must surely have been possible to compromise on this issue. For example, a distinction could be made between those who come with pre-agreed employment and those who come opportunistically looking for work. Freedom of movement for the former should satisfy the single market test. An alternative approach would have been some kind of 'brake' of the kind David Cameron sought but failed to secure pre-Brexit.

CONCLUSIONS

1. Politically, it is not possible to sustain the principle of 'free movement of labour' for EU nationals or, in a wider sense, to argue for unrestricted immigration. The economics broadly favour liberal immigration, but the arguments are not one sided or clear-cut.
2. One simple and obvious step is to stop counting overseas students as part of 'net immigration'. Restrictions are self-harming for the UK and there is little evidence of public concern about overseas students.
3. It is commonly argued that areas under stress from high immigration need extra help from government. There may be value in this approach in some instances. But the greatest opposition to immigration is often to be found in areas with little immigration and those under the greatest demographic pressure will be London boroughs, which also see the economic benefits, rather than depressed regions of the UK.
4. The Brexit negotiations will have to produce an outcome which enables the government to demonstrate that migration from the EU is 'under control' (and that is a reasonable objective). But this could be achieved by, for example, limiting 'free movement of labour' to those who have pre-agreed jobs.

THE MORNING AFTER THE NIGHT BEFORE

What does Brexit mean for British identity?

Stephen Green

I woke up very early that Friday morning after the Brexit vote in June last year. The news was a shock and sleep vanished instantly. And shock was what many others I know felt too. I and they had voted to remain. Over the following days, the mood – in me and around me – was a swirling mix of disbelief, dismay and anger. Even the leavers among my friends and acquaintances were surprised. And it became clear very quickly that few people in either business or government had much idea what Brexit would mean in specific terms. For a while, some remainers – who seemed to become more passionate in defeat than they had been at any stage in the campaign – pinned their hopes on the petition for a new referendum. Some still hope that it may not in the end come to an actual Brexit – that a new grand bargain which in effect changes the nature of the EU will allow continued British membership on a basis which is more acceptable to the British people. Others – both leavers who had been nervous about whether they had done the right thing by their children (as one father of a nine year old confessed to me), and remainers who have been relieved that so far at least the sky has not fallen in – have become more relaxed, more comfortable with the new reality, and more optimistic that Britain will find a reasonable modus vivendi with its European neighbours.

We shall see. Much of the campaigning was a cacophony of exaggeration and lies, some of which still rankles deeply. Not much of it did justice to the complexity of the case for or against membership of the EU – a case which was inevitably multi-layered, involving issues of sovereignty, of migration and border control, of commercial trade offs, and of geopolitics. With varying degrees of clarity and emphasis, debates on all these themes did feature in the national discussion leading up to the vote. But they have not gone away or been conclusively resolved by the vote. All it did was close off the status quo ante. Now we are in a sort of limbo, which could well last for some years.

But whatever the eventual outcome, a critical question we need to ask ourselves is: what does the vote tell us about what sort of society we are? Why, in fact, was it a shock? For a remainer like myself it was certainly a disappointment. And I admit that it was also a surprise, because I went to bed the previous day thinking it would probably be all right on the night. But why such a deep shock? After all, the opinion polls had clearly shown that it was neck and neck. The result was entirely within the range of expectations – within the margin of error of virtually every poll over at least the previous fortnight or so.

It was a shock because we had not understood how divided the country was. Old against young, provincial against metropolitan, Scotland and London against much of the rest of England and Wales. The overall result was close; but few of the results by area were close – most were strongly one way or the other. Apart from anything else, this referendum displayed the extent of the distance between the British establishment on the one hand – in which I include Westminster and Whitehall, the City, big business, academia and the professional middle classes – and much of the rest of England and Wales (though not Scotland) on the other. And that has rung alarm bells, as indeed it should.

It was also a shock – in fact, it was deeply shaming – to see the upsurge in racial abuse and violence which followed the result. For me this was not just a matter of statistics and of stories in the media:

I know people personally who experienced wholly gratuitous abuse or were made to feel uncomfortable and unwelcome – and these are people who have lived in Britain for years.

You learn by reflecting on the past, and by recognising individual and collective failures. There is plenty of scope for debate about what exactly those failures are – and they certainly include all the sins of omission and commission which have resulted in a society so unequal in life chances, and in which many feel so resentful of what they see as so alien. The financial and economic crisis of recent years clearly played its part – and bankers, of whom I was one, have much to atone for in that story. But deeper than this lies the whole failure over decades to invest properly in the country's societal future – above all through education and training fit for the purpose of enhancing life chances. Instead, we have benefitted from an economic growth path which has allowed the country to live beyond its means by running a yawning trade deficit, and – in the absence of material growth of labour productivity – we have found it easy to fill gaps in the skills base through immigration.

We should also note the short-sightedness and indeed dishonesty of the British political class (of all colours) ever since the years after the second world war, when the founders of the European project sought to create a new European order in the aftermath of catastrophe. How different the EU, which so many of us love to hate and to blame for all our ills, could have been. How much better it could have been, if only Britain had engaged wholeheartedly from the start and led the shaping of it, at a time when Britain's influence would have been dominant. How much better for Europe; how much better the options could have been for the people of this country too. But our forebears were still at that time fixated by empire.

Which leads me to an even deeper question that we must ask ourselves. For if we just focus on the policies and practices of the British establishment over the last few decades – important though it undoubtedly is to do so – then we will miss some of the most uncomfortable truths about ourselves. For what has not been recognised clearly enough is that underlying all the sound and fury of the Brexit debate was a question – whether or not fully acknowledged – about identity. Do we think of ourselves as Europeans, and if so did this mean that we should see our destiny as bound up with the European Union? Or are we different, special and perfectly capable of finding our own way in the world? Who are we, who call ourselves British?

I believe that we British have not been living wholly honestly with our past. Whether we feel we are members of the establishment or whether we feel alienated from it and mistrustful of it – in either case, too many of us have lived for too long with a general sense that we can be proud of our history and of the role Britain has played in European and in global history.

And indeed, there is much to be proud of: yes, we did stand alone against the evil of the Third Reich in May 1940. Yes, we did bring a halt to Napoleon's vaulting ambition at Waterloo (albeit with the crucial help of the Prussians). Yes, it was Britons who led the campaign to abolish the slave trade. Yes, we have had a continuously adjusting constitution ever since the signing of the Magna Carta which has given us the mother of parliaments. Yes, our common law, evolved over the centuries and upheld by an independent judiciary is – in the words of W. S. Gilbert – "the true embodiment of everything that's excellent". Yes, we are the heirs of Shakespeare and our language has become the *lingua franca* of the planet.

But the fact is that there are other things in the scales too. For this was also the country whose foreign policy from the 19th century onwards was conducted with what can only – from our present vantage point – be described as breath-taking arrogance and selfishness. What do we make of the famous dictum of Lord Palmerston that Britain has no permanent allies, only permanent interests? Not only was this wrong even in its own terms (he clearly defined the British presence in India as a permanent interest): but more generally, it reduces all international relationships to pure contracts. How much wiser (and indeed, ironically appropriate in this context) were the famous words of John Donne over two centuries earlier: no man is an island entire of itself, but every man a piece of the continent. He meant this in the context of individual human relationships;

he meant that we are not just autonomous individuals, but that we are connected deeply, that we are 'involved in mankind'. But as individuals we are members of communities, of societies, and – as matters stand, at least – citizens of nations. What he said applies not only to individuals but also to the communities, the societies, the nations we are part of.

And still more basically: where does the notion of Britain itself come from? Answer: it was the creation of an 18th century establishment – both English and Scottish – which closed down the Scottish and Irish parliaments and which led to the over-centralisation of national life in London. No one thought of themselves as British before that time. It was, to be sure, the beginning of a vibrant period – a time of industrial inventiveness, scientific progress, enlightenment philosophy, missionary zeal and trade. British energy brought success, and success brought pride in a navy which could reach anywhere in the world to further and protect its interests.

But it is also true that the concept of Britannia became the icon of a 19th century imperialism whose record is a good deal more mixed than many of us are comfortable in recognising – as any Indian or Chinese person, for example, can remind those of us who choose to forget some of its darker episodes. Likewise, the history of British involvement in the affairs of the Middle East from the beginning of the 20th century onwards is filled with cynicism and duplicity – not to mention moments of sheer folly.

And if that is not enough, we need to remember – as we fret about the fragility of the United Kingdom and about a possible breakaway by the Scots – that the United Kingdom has broken up before. Ireland was in effect Britain's longest running and worst colonial experience. No one can read about the greed, insensitivity and often outright brutality in the behaviour of both English and Scottish interests in Ireland over the 400 years leading up to the first world war without a sense of shame and of tragedy. It is shocking how little attention was given during the referendum debates to the effect of it all in Ireland. Much has changed, of course, over the last 100 years. In particular, the EU has given Ireland a new place in the world and a new self-esteem. And the Good Friday agreement planted a new, vulnerable tree of opportunity, constantly in need of protection and nurture. Yet somehow, the British go on treating the island of Ireland as an afterthought.

All of this may seem a long way from the Brexit question. But it is not. We live with the consequences still: the concentrated establishment in London, and the assumption that we have a special role in the world, given to us by a history that the world ought to admire. Just as we live with what the vote told us about our own society, so we live with what it tells us about who we think we are. At home we have walked by too often on the other side: on the world stage we have been blind to the beam in our own eye.

This may seem harsh. But in our individual lives we do not hesitate to acknowledge that spiritual maturity comes through honest self-analysis, recognition and renewal. I think that is true of nations too. Other European nations, of course, have reason enough to acknowledge this truth. But we do too. Brexit is one of the those history-making crossroads which – whatever else it means – gives us occasion for a reflection which, if honest, cannot help involving introspection and a renewed commitment to the common good. That is now our challenge: to be honest about our history, to invest in our people, to be good neighbours in Europe, to be open to the world.

THE FAILURE OF NEOLIBERALISM

PARTNERS FOR A NEW KIND OF GROWTH

Progressive politicians must come together with business and trade unions to build an economy of purpose

Stephen Kinnock

There can be no doubt that 2016 was a watershed year, marked (much like other pivotal years such as 1929, 1945, 1979 and 1989), by an eruption of underlying political and economic tensions that had been simmering away for years.

The year of 1929 saw the Wall Street crash and the beginning of the Great Depression, sparking America's New Deal, Europe's totalitarianism, and finally war. In 1945 we saw the progressive postwar consensus resolution of that crash, as politics re-invented itself to build a new economy and society. The unravelling of that consensus began in 1979, both through the emergence of Thatcherism and Reaganism and through Gorbachev's election to the Politburo. The next pivotal year was 1989, as Tiananmen, Solidarity and the fall of the Berlin Wall seemed to indicate that liberalism, democracy and the free market were set fair to reign supreme, forever more. Indeed, 1989 appeared to mark 'The End of History', as Francis Fukuyama so memorably wrote.

Last year represents the political reckoning for the potent cocktail of hope and hubris that was uncorked in 1989. The untamed, unfettered, deregulated forces of globalisation and free-market capitalism that were set loose on the world in the 1990s conspired to create and inflate the various bubbles that eventually led to the crash of 2008. The existing order staggered along for a few years after 2009, but with the benefit of hindsight, the catastrophic fragility of the system should have been clear for all to see. Its foundations had in fact been cracking for decades, and 2016 is simply the year in which the ground finally gave way beneath our feet. The financial crash of 2008 was the earthquake that shook the world, and the electoral upheavals of 2016 have simply been the consequences of the political tsunami that followed in its wake.

The British economy is a prime example of the fragility that has come to define modern capitalism. At first glance things look fairly positive: relatively strong growth, unemployment down, inflation under control. But scratch below the surface and a very different picture emerges (made all the more acute by Brexit): we have a gaping trade deficit, low productivity, ballooning personal debt, creaking infrastructure, an over-reliance on financial services, and the distribution of wealth and resources slopes dangerously towards London and the south east.

The weakness at the heart of our system is that we have lost touch with the first principles that should govern an economy of purpose, and the absence of these core principles has created a vacuum into which the forces of reaction and nationalism have duly stepped. What follows is therefore my attempt to re-affirm the core principles of progressive capitalism, and to then set out three policy area examples to illustrate how those principles could be put into practice.

BUILDING AN ECONOMY OF PURPOSE

Growth has lifted billions of people out of poverty, and it has also improved quality of life for billions more. The market economy is the most effective driver of growth, bar none. Progressive politics must always, therefore, resolutely defend the basic tenets of the market economy.

But we must also recognise that the model is broken: the benefits of growth are not being spread equitably, inequality is endemic, and 2016 has demonstrated, in the starkest possible terms, just how fragile the system is.

If we are to fix our broken model we must get back to first principles, which means re-examining and re-defining what the economy is actually for. In my view, this re-definition should rest on five core principles, meaning that the economy must:

- provide enough money for people to live on, and to feel secure in their lives;
- speak to people's dignity: that is to say work must not be demeaning and must support a sense of purpose and resilience;
- speak to people's ambitions, delivering the opportunity for personal and community advancement;
- enhance our common endeavor: we levy taxes on individuals and businesses so that we can deliver public services and correct for market failures;
- operate within our planet's boundaries.

Through partnership

Having defined the economy of purpose, the question then is how to go about shaping it? Here, 'partnership' should be the watchword.

Change does not happen in a vacuum, it is informed by specific interests, objectives and outlooks – all of them human, but not all of them benign. The job of progressive politics is not simply to react and adapt to change; it is to become an engine for change. We know that globalisation, de-industrialisation and the technology revolution have radically altered the world, and we also know that successive postwar governments have failed to harness those forces and channel them into equitable, sustainable and balanced outcomes for ordinary working people.

No single group can hope to tackle these challenges in isolation. In our deeply interlinked and interdependent world, the connections between policymaking, business planning and civil society agendas are almost seamless. But all too often politicians have attempted to shape the political economy from inside the ivory towers of Westminster, and business leaders have tended to see the creation of value in the narrowest possible terms, as opposed to engaging with society at large.

During my time at the World Economic Forum, I saw the power of cross-sectoral collaboration, and it left me in no doubt that if we are to deliver the radical changes to our broken model that are so urgently required, then we must do so through partnership.

Applying the 'partners for a new kind of growth' approach, I explore how we should build a modern manufacturing renaissance, reshape corporate governance, and re-invent our state pension system.

BUILDING A MODERN MANUFACTURING RENAISSANCE

In 1970, manufacturing accounted for one third of the British economy; in 2015 it stands at barely 10 per cent. The dramatic decline of our manufacturing sector is the root cause of three deep-seated structural weaknesses in the British economy, namely: the productivity crisis, the trade deficit, and the lack of balance across regions and sectors.

The deeply imbalanced nature of the British economy is arguably the most serious of these three structural weaknesses, because an economy that lacks balance is, by definition, less resilient. It is essential that the government focuses on rebalancing the economy away from services and towards modern manufacturing, so that our economy becomes more resilient and therefore better able to weather the stormy waters of globalisation, the uncertainties of

Brexit, and the chilling effect of Donald Trump's anti-trade presidency of the US.

The driving purpose of the government's emerging industrial strategy must, therefore, be to rebalance the British economy by building a modern manufacturing renaissance.

Let's be clear: 21st century manufacturing is not metal-bashing – far from it. Take the steel industry, which is the beating heart of the economy in my Aberavon constituency, thanks to the Port Talbot steelworks. The fact is that the majority of the steel produced in the UK today did not even exist 15 years ago. Far from being a 'sunset industry', steel and the vast majority of UK manufacturing is at the leading edge of industrial innovation and technological change. Or take the manufacture of pharmaceuticals, where coding and the use of data to improve the product/service are core skill requirements, thus encompassing a far broader sweep of the workforce.

Let us also recall that the distinction between manufacturing and services is blurring. For example, Rolls Royce might be considered more of a services firm today, given that its revenues are increasingly derived from the servicing of its engines rather the selling of them. Modern manufacturing elides the difference with services, as the most successful businesses often offer packages that involve making things and then offering long-term wrap-around services for what they produce.

If it is to build a modern manufacturing renaissance, the government must come forward with a coherent industrial strategy. Such a strategy will entail a number of elements, including:

Skills

Successive governments have tinkered incessantly with technical education qualifications and standards, to such an extent that the sector is in a mess. It is essential that the new Institute for Apprenticeships and Technical Education is given the time and investment required for success.

Innovation

The UK has a strong research capability and a world-class community of universities, but we struggle when it comes to driving our new ideas and technologies to market. The progressive critique of Conservative industrial policy since 2010 should, therefore, focus on the swingeing cuts to the innovation budget – and particularly Innovate UK and the catapults. Spending on R&D is just 1.7% of GDP, against an EU average of 2.6%. A new compact is now required between government and business, to take spending on R&D to the OECD average of 3% of GDP.

Energy

There is a pressing need for a 10-year plan that lays out the investment path required to build a secure, competitively priced and clean energy supply. It is completely unacceptable and unsustainable that energy intensive industries in the UK pay 40-45% more for their electricity than do their continental European competitors.

Infrastructure

The UK's inadequate transport and digital infrastructure is a major contributor to the chasm that exists between London and the rest of the country. There is an urgent need for long-term infrastructure plan, which has to be at the heart of the modern manufacturing renaissance.

Finance

The UK's banking system is fundamentally skewed towards the stimulation of private consumption, asset value inflation and personal debt. A new financial support system for manufacturing is needed, and it should take inspiration from Germany's *spaarkassen*: truly local banking that is embedded in the fabric of the regional economy, focused exclusively on lending to startups and SMEs in the manufacturing sector.

Partnership must underpin each and every element of the modern manufacturing renaissance. The strategy and plan must be co-created by business, government, trade unions and communities, so that they are rooted in reality and reflect the real needs.

RE-SHAPING CORPORATE GOVERNANCE

There is a palpable lack of trust between business and society. Take the referendum campaign. We saw 1,200 business leaders, together employing 1.75 million people – including 51 of the FTSE 100 – appeal to the public not to sever our 43-year relationship with Europe, and not to risk job prospects and pensions funds. But their advice was ignored by a decisive majority of the electorate.

There can be little doubt that the breakdown in trust between business and society has been building for decades, but it was the 2008 financial crisis that took levels of outrage to unprecedented levels. The events leading up to the collapse of Lehman Brothers put business firmly on the wrong side of the public, and trust went off the cliff.

So, we must now strain every sinew to rebuild the trust that has been lost, and business has a vital role to play in this process. A vital element of this will be acting to bring an end to 'quarterly capitalism', so we must regulate and legislate where appropriate to build a more long-term, investment-driven business culture. For too many boardrooms, the delivery of fast-buck profits to shareholders takes priority over all other considerations, including investment in skills, technology and R&D. To address this we will require a new deal between shareholders, companies, and their workforce, as well as a new deal between the public and private sectors. The reshaping of company law is a necessity, but we must also look at reshaping ownership structures in a manner that empowers managers to think and plan for the long term.

Reshaping corporate governance should be based on amending the Companies Act to include the following:

- A national public interest clause, as a precondition for foreign takeovers, ensuring that the national interest is considered alongside shareholder interest;
- Triple bottom line reporting: people, planet, profit. Companies should not be allowed to incorporate unless their declared purpose strikes a balance between their societal, environmental and financial obligations. This new balanced-purpose precondition should be a statutory measure, and would form the benchmark against which the performance of all company directors would be managed. It would also be deployed to block takeover bids where the leadership team feels that the takeover being proposed would not further the company's balanced-purpose mission;
- Rewrite article 172 of the Companies Act, to make it clear that company directors are not only required to deliver value for shareholders, but also to society at large. Article 172, as it currently stands, hardwires shareholder primacy into the statutory purpose of the company, whereas shareholder value should be placed on equal footing with societal and environmental value.

The best businesses get it. Emerging trends such as the rise of the aware consumer, increased transparency and the need to attract talent to a business model that inspires pride are combining to lead businesses to understand the need to place ethics and responsibility at the heart of their operations. This represents a real opportunity for progressive politicians to engage with the private sector, to build support for legislative and regulatory reforms, as partners for a new kind of growth.

RE-INVENTING OUR STATE PENSION: THE ANDEAN MODEL

In his interim report, the independent pension reviewer, John Cridland, warned that the state pension bill is set to increase by 39%, to £152bn a year, by 2028. Part of this is down to the triple lock, and part is down to demographics as we become an increasingly ageing society. The triple lock ensures that state pensions increase by the inflation rate, the growth in average earnings, or 2.5%, whichever is the highest, and it is a policy that is already making a challenging outlook all the more acute. If, for example, we were to experience a period of deflation, in which both earnings and prices were falling, increasing pensions by 2.5% would be a challenge for the state. Cridland's review, however, is focused on the age threshold at which one is entitled to receive the state pension, and the indication appears to be that he will recommend that age increases be accelerated beyond what is originally planned.

But this has been the limited scope of political public policy discussions about pensions: increasing the age of receipt and questioning the viability of the triple lock. Such reforms, however, amount to little more than tinkering, and will do nothing to build the kind of economy and society that can provide for us all through retirement. The need for radical reform could not be greater, as the role of the state in pension provision looks set to increase for three reasons: first, the danger of private schemes defaulting and overwhelming the PPF; and second, the challenge of the self-employed. Almost 4.6 million people work for themselves in Britain, and the DWP estimates that around 22% of them, that is just under 1 million people, have no pension whatsoever, meaning they must rely on their own savings and the state pension; and third, the impact of demographic changes on the dependency ratio.

And it is this third challenge, that of the dependency ratio, that poses the greatest challenges to the viability of our pension system. Since the 1980s, the number of UK residents aged over 90 has tripled, and that trend will only continue. This, coupled with working-age population changes that may result from Brexit, will put further pressure on the dependency ratio. The old age dependency ratio (OADR) measures the number of people of state pension age (SPA) and over for every 1,000 people of working age (16 to SPA) and provides an idea of the relationship between working and pensioner populations. The OADR held steady at around 300 from the

1980s to 2006, but rose in 2007-09 as many female 'baby boomers' reached SPA. In the absence of any increases to SPA, it would reach 487 by 2039; but, as a result of planned SPA increases taking place between 2010 and 2046, it is expected that for every 1,000 people of working age in 2039 there will be 370 people of SPA[1]. Put simply: the increase in the OADR means there will be fewer people of working age to support a larger population over SPA. That is a problem that cannot simply be resolved by increasing the age at which one receives their SPA, and may, instead, require us to move away from our 'pay-as-you-go' system towards one that is 'fully funded'.

The appeal of moving towards a fully funded model is that such a system is less severely affected by demographic changes. While a pay-as-you-go scheme relies upon current workers funding current retirees – meaning you need more people paying in than taking out of the system – a funded scheme is financed out of the contributions made by pensioners themselves throughout their working life. Workers pay into a pension pot which, at any one time, has enough money in it to finance their future pensions.

One potential fully funded state pension system is the so-called Andean model, in which retirement income is linked to cumulative savings rather than a fixed amount. Replicating such a system would also involve a means tested 'top up', guaranteeing a minimum income higher than current levels. The appeal of this system is that it would ensure a better deal for the worst off: maximising the value of existing savings and using means-testing to top up payments to a level more sufficient than the current £155 a week. One approach to funding this top-up system could be to establish a National Pension Commission (NPC), modeled on the Low Pay Commission. The NPC would be tasked with setting what it considers to be a 'national living pension'. All UK residents would pay a flat rate of their salary into their pension. At retirement age, any funds in excess of the 'national living pension', as set by the NPC, would be redeployed into a 'pension solidarity fund'. This fund could be used as the

---

1.   http://visual.ons.gov.uk/uk-perspectives-2016-the-changing-uk-population/

mechanism for topping up all those who, at retirement, had accrued savings that were below the level of the 'national living pension'.

The second benefit of the Andean model is that it would create a system that matches the expectations most have. Many savers believe our current system is a funded, rather than pay-as-you-go system, and so the transparency of a funded scheme – workers know that what they pay in will come back to them upon retirement – is a further benefit.

The great challenge, however, of moving towards a funded system is in the transition from one to another system. There is no denying that this will produce some relative winners and losers. However, this could be mitigated with a 'pre-fund' payment: a capital amount equivalent to what savers would have 'earned' through their national insurance contribution, with the revenue for this funded by a special issue of government bonds. Yes, this would mean an increase in government debt, but it would, in reality, be a conversion of off-the-balance-sheet liabilities into an increase in headline debt. This is more transparent and accountable, as well as being more sustainable for Britain in the long term. Conversion payments could be introduced to alleviate intergenerational wealth inequalities in a means tested manner.

As well as creating a more sustainable, fair and transparent system, this reform could also bring about meaningful benefits to corporate governance. The conversion payment involved in establishing the system would probably involve bonds being sold by pension managers to buy equities – dramatically changing the ownership mix of UK plc, and thereby giving every UK citizen a direct stake in the United Kingdom's largest companies. So in addition to helping resolve the demographic crunch our pension system faces, moving towards a funded system could also play a role in reforming corporate culture and building a stakeholder society.

These ideas are at an embryonic stage. However, it is clear is that this debate must be had, and it must urgently be had in partnership between the state, savers, pensioners, and businesses.

CONCLUSION

The great strength of the market economy is its dynamism – driven by the way in which it flexes to respond to market forces and consumer demand. However, unless urgent action is taken to fix our broken model, the market economy risks becoming an increasingly discredited and distrusted system.

The failed European response to the crash of 1929 led directly to the rise of demagogues and populists. Progressives, now and always, must think and act radically, to fix the broken foundations of our growth model. The time for incremental tinkering is over. We have seen where that has taken us. We must, as partners for a new kind of growth, seize this moment to reshape capitalism and make it fit for the 21st century.

WHAT IS THE ROLE OF THE STATE IN THE ECONOMY?

Progressive capitalism and a look beyond the third way

David Sainsbury

The fundamental question that political economy seeks to answer is 'what is the role of the state in the economy?' If one believes in the highly mathematical, neoclassical theory of economic growth, which today dominates the economics profession, then the role of the state is inevitably very limited. If one holds the view that, with the exception of a few minor market failures, the market economy works perfectly if left alone, then inevitably one sees the role of the state as a minor one.

But increasingly, I believe, policymakers are coming to understand that neoclassical economic growth theory is unable to explain why in the past the economies of some countries have grown and others have declined, or why in the last few years the rate of economic growth in almost all developed countries has fallen. They are also coming to realise that because neoclassical growth theory has such an unrealistic model of the economy that it is able to give little help to policymakers who want to raise the rate of economic growth in their countries.

The reason why the neoclassical theory of economic growth has so little explanatory value is not difficult to see, as it is based on four assumptions which economic observation shows to be unrealistic. It has, of course, been argued that it does not matter if the assumptions on which an economic theory is based are in some way unrealistic, as long as the theory makes accurate predictions. This argument would have some force if neoclassical growth theory produced accurate predictions, or explained the past growth performance of countries, but clearly it does not.

The first assumption of neoclassical economic growth theory that is unrealistic is that firms operate in a world of perfect competition. In this world, the entrepreneur cannot influence the price of what he produces. He literally reads, or sees on his iPhone, what the market is willing to pay. He is a price-taker rather than a price-maker. But such perfect competition exists in only a few mining and agricultural markets. In most markets, firms seek to gain a competitive advantage over their rivals so that they can grow their businesses.

The second unrealistic assumption of neoclassical economic growth theory is that technology is a factor of production which is freely and instantly available to all companies. In a more realistic version of this assumption, firms, knowing the probabilities of success of different R&D strategies, have to invest to acquire new technologies. This is not only a very unrealistic model of the innovation process, it is also one which it is difficult to reconcile with a world of perfect competition. Why would any firm want to invest in R&D to produce a better product if it is going to compete in a world of perfect competition?

The third unrealistic assumption is that all firms have the same technological and organisational capabilities, and that models of the economy can be built up on the basis of 'the representative firm'. Such a model of the firm has no room in it for the entrepreneur, and it is one of the ironies of modern growth theory that a theory of economic growth much beloved by entrepreneurs has no role for entrepreneurs in it.

The final unrealistic assumption of neoclassical economic growth theory is that institutions have no impact on the performance of firms, and that as a result firms operate in a flat world where it does not matter where they locate. But as Michael Porter wrote in *The Competitive Advantage of Nations*:

Competitive advantage is created and sustained through a highly localised process. Differences in national economic structures, values, cultures, institutions and histories contribute profoundly to competitive success. The role of the home nation seems to be as strong as or stronger than ever.

These four unrealistic assumptions of neoclassical growth theory are enthusiastically embraced by economists not, I suspect, because they believe them to be true, but because they remove from economic growth theory all the complex and dynamic processes, such as innovation, learning and the creation of competitive advantage, which make it difficult mathematically to model.

They also remove all sector-specific information from their models of economic growth, with the result that the economy is seen as a single entity, although if we look at a country's rate of economic growth at any moment of time we see that it is made up of some sectors which are growing fast, some of which are declining and some of which are flatlining.

The unrealistic nature of the neoclassical model of economic growth means that it has little explanatory value, is unable to provide much help to policymakers who want to increase the rate of economic growth of their countries, and cannot be used to define the role of the state in the economy. We, therefore, badly need a new theory.

Where should we look for the new ideas on which a new theory of economic growth can be built? I believe the answer to this question is to be found in the work of those empirical economists in the Schumpeterian tradition who look at the growth dynamics of sectors such as pharmaceuticals, machine tools and telecommunications in different countries.[1] Their world is a very different one from the world of neoclassical economics. Instead of being based on a set of unrealistic assumptions, their theory of economic growth is based

---

1. Malerba, Franco, editor, *Sectoral Systems of Innovation*, Cambridge University Press, 2004.

on a set of observations that are almost the exact opposite of the assumptions of neoclassical economics.

They argue that we do not live in a world of perfect competition but one in which competitive advantage drives economic growth. They also better understand the role of technology in creating competitive advantage. In their world, technology is usually sector specific, and firms have to put resources into creating it or learning it from more advanced countries, a process which takes time.

Firms are also not all the same, and the capabilities they build up play a critical role in enabling them to take advantage of the market opportunities that appear or which they create. They also understand that the creation of competitive advantage does not take place in a vacuum, but is greatly affected by the institutions of the country where the firm is located. The world is, therefore, not a flat one where all firms, no matter where they are located, have an equal opportunity to make innovations.

If we accept the idea that it is competitive advantage that drives the growth of firms, then the obvious next question is how do firms innovate?

The best way to answer this question is to look at the large volume of business school research on corporate strategy and competitive advantage, where there is a long line of thinking that argues that the competitive advantage of firms is driven by a capabilities/market opportunity dynamic.

According to this theory, an opportunity to create a competitive advantage emerges as the result of a latent demand for a new product or the development of a new technology, and an entrepreneur then uses the capabilities of his firm to take advantage of this new opportunity.

For example, the entrepreneur, Steve Jobs, saw that there was a large latent demand for personal computers, and he formed a company, Apple, with the necessary capabilities to exploit the technology he found, at places such as Xerox's Palo Alto Research Centre, to meet that demand.

This capability/market opportunity dynamic model of economic growth can, I believe, be used to explain why particular countries grew fast at particular times in the past, and can also be of use to politicians and policymakers who are seeking to raise the rate of economic growth in their country. If, for example, we wish to explain why the growth of the cotton industry played such a large role in the Industrial Revolution in Great Britain, or why the dye industry grew so fast in Germany at the end of the 19th century, or why the car industry expanded rapidly first of all in the US, then, I believe a capability/market opportunity dynamic provides the best explanation.

Progressive politicians and policymakers believe that the market economy is the best way to achieve prosperity but that history shows that the state can play a constructive role in the economy, enabling greater economic growth and a more socially just society. The capability/market opportunity theory of economic growth can help them define what this enabling role should be.

If we want the state to play a valuable enabling role in the economy, we need to be clear first of all that we are not talking about an entrepreneurial or directive role for the state. In the past, leftwing governments have too frequently seen the role of government as being an entrepreneurial one in which the government decides which are the industries and firms into which capital should flow.

As has been shown again and again, this is a disastrous way for capital to be allocated in an economy. Entrepreneurial decisions need to be taken by entrepreneurs who can identify the opportunities that exist in a particular segment of industry, and who know whether a firm exists, or can be created, which has the capabilities to take advantage of those opportunities.

The last people who should make such decisions are politicians and civil servants, who do not have either the knowledge of markets or firm capabilities to make them, and who, if they do make them, invariably make them for the wrong economic reasons, such as to promote national prestige or because it is thought that they will bring employment to an area of high unemployment.

There are, however, two vitally important ways in which the state can constructively support economic growth. The first is by funding the public goods that play a critical role in helping firms create competitive advantage. The most important of these is the funding of basic research in a country. The funding of basic research cannot be left to industry, as the risks that nothing of commercial value will be produced from the funding of a piece of basic research are far too great for any one firm, and no one firm is in a position to appropriate all of the added value which flows from a breakthrough in basic research.

As well as funding basic research, recent decades have also shown that the government needs to fund, at least partially, the next stage of the R&D cycle after the basic research stage. This is the demonstration of the commercial feasibility of new technologies, and the end product of this phase is 'generic technology' or 'proof of concept'. The failure of governments to partially fund generic technologies can contribute significantly to the high risks faced by the private sector when introducing radical new technologies, risks which have come to be labelled 'the valley of death'.

It is well known that the generic technology which enabled the internet to be developed in the US was largely funded by the Defense Advanced Research Projects Agency. But much of the generic technology that was of vital importance in supporting the growth of the biotechnology industry in the US was also funded by the National Institutes of Health. In fact, it has been argued that the generic technologies of most of the industries in which the US now leads the world were developed by federal agencies of the US government of one type or another.

The second area where government needs to play an enabling role is in the design of the three key institutions that are of critical importance to firms seeking to create new competitive advantages. They are a country's system of education and training, its system of corporate governance, and its national system of innovation.

The reason why the laws and rules which regulate the relationships between individuals and organisations in these three institutions are needed follows from the production theory of economic growth I have outlined. In that theory, the way companies are managed is clearly very important, and the system of corporate governance is, therefore, a policy area which has to be on the agenda of government.

Equally, the capabilities of a firm depend to a large extent on the education and training system of the country where it is located, while its ability to create technological opportunities, and take advantage of them, depends on its national system of innovation.

The state has to play a key role in the design of these institutions because the different groups who are affected by them will have conflicting views as to how they should operate, and if left alone will not necessarily produce the design which is best for the country. And in the past in the UK, the design of these institutions has not been as good as it should have been.

If we take, first of all, the technical education system in the UK, it is over 100 years since it was pointed out that it was not as good as that of Germany, and since the second world war there have been many attempts to improve it.

But these have all failed because they have not put in place what, if one looks at the best technical education systems in the world, are the key components of an effective system of technical education. They are, first of all, a well-understood national system of qualifications that works in the marketplace. Young people will only work hard to get a qualification if employers give priority to individuals who possess it. It is also necessary to have an effective system for funding students while they are training, and modern facilities and competent and inspiring teachers.

The UK today has none of these features. The system of qualifications is very complex, with over 13,000 qualifications available for 16–18-year-olds. These often provide little value for either individuals or employers. There are not enough good quality apprenticeships at the right level available to young people, and the technical education pathway is poorly funded so that there are not modern facilities or competent and inspiring teachers. As a result, UK industry suffers from a serious shortage of technicians in industry at a time when over 400,000 16–24-year-olds are unemployed.

The second key UK institution which is in need of reform is the system of corporate governance. In recent years many investment managers have ceased to exercise their rights as shareholders, and as a result we have had 'capitalism without owners'.

A major attempt to reform the UK's system of corporate governance was made with the issuance of the Cadbury Code of 1992. This voluntary code of conduct contained two main provisions. First, the chairman's role should in principle be separate from that of the chief executive, and, second, the non-executive directors should be given more power. Moreover the non-executive directors should be able to demonstrate independence from management.

While the issuance of the Cadbury Code has resulted in some improvements, it has arguably made the overall situation worse. The non-executive directors have been effectively appointed by the management of their companies, and have not, therefore, been prepared to stand up to them when they believe that the company is not being managed as it should be.

As a result, complex remuneration systems for directors linked to the value of their company's shares have been introduced. This has led to the remuneration of top executives sky-rocketing upwards, often unrelated to the performance of their companies. These remuneration systems have also seemingly had the effect of incentivising chief executives to manipulate the value of the shares of their companies, by using the spare cash their companies generate to buy back shares, rather than investing it so as to create new competitive advantages in the future. The reform of the country's corporate governance system should, therefore, once again be on the agenda of government.

The third UK institution which needs to be improved is the national system of innovation. This was defined by Chris Freeman in 1987 as "the network of institutions in the public and private sectors whose activities and interactions initiate, import and diffuse new technologies". It involves factors such as a country's organisations for the funding of science and technology research; its universities, research institutes and company laboratories; its public purchasing of innovative products and services; and its use of tax incentives to encourage innovation.

The Labour government that came into power in 1997 made this area of policy a priority and achieved some success with the setting up of the Higher Education Innovation Fund to encourage technology transfer from the universities, the Small Business Research Initiative to stimulate innovative procurement by government, and the Technology Strategy Board (TSB) to manage the government's collaborative research programmes.

The coalition government that came into power in 2010 built upon the work of the Labour government, but with the election of a Conservative government in 2015, government policy went into reverse. The budget of the TSB (now named Innovate UK) was cut back, and the government appeared no longer to believe in the value of innovation policy.

It can be seen then that the new thinking on economic growth defines an important enabling role for the state in the economy. But if the government is to carry out this new role effectively it needs to build up its capacity to do so.

In a number of areas, such as corporate governance, the same policy should apply to all companies, but in those relating to technology, innovation and training, as well as those relating to regulations and trade, there is a sectoral dimension to government policies. This means the government needs to work with industry associations or sector councils to make certain that its policies are related to the needs of individual sectors.

If we want to define clearly the role that the progressive state should take in the economy we should not seek to find a third way by splitting the difference between laissez-faire capitalism and the socialist planning of industry. Instead we should seek to understand the capabilities/market opportunity dynamic, which drives economic growth, and then use that understanding to define the role the enabling state should play.

A BROKEN SYSTEM

Why has neoliberalism failed to produce inclusive growth?

Andrew Gamble

Neoliberalism has never been a single doctrine or programme. It has many different roots and few neoliberals have ever accepted the label as an accurate one. But neoliberal ideas, broadly defined, have been very influential in the last few decades, and helped establish a new policy regime and a dominant common-sense about economic policy. It became the dominant framework of ideas in political economy, and in important respects it remains so. Since the 2008 financial crash, however, and the long slow stuttering recovery which has followed, a fierce light has been shone on neoliberalism and the many tensions within it. Like Keynesianism before it, neoliberalism has developed its own pathologies and has become an amalgam of unstable forces, both economic and political, which threaten to destroy it.

One of the greatest tensions in neoliberalism has been its promise to deliver inclusive growth and the marked acceleration of inequality under its rule. Neoliberalism rose to prominence during the 1970s' era of stagflation as a critique of the Keynesian and social democratic consensus, which it was argued had led to an impasse of no growth, accelerating inflation and rising unemployment. Major policy and institutional changes were necessary to restore prosperity. The catalyst for this was the breakdown of the postwar international monetary system, the floating of all the major currencies and the determination of the United States to find new instruments to enforce financial discipline through the international institutions it controlled, particularly the International Monetary Fund and the World Bank. National governments were forced to give up a great deal of sovereignty and adopt new monetary and fiscal rules for managing their economies. This was the beginning of what came to be known as globalisation and the Washington consensus. National governments varied in their responses. Some embraced the new order enthusiastically, others resisted it as far as they could, but all were forced to adjust to it.

At the heart of neoliberalism was a series of prescriptions for restoring economic growth. These included reducing public spending in order to reduce taxation, making labour markets more flexible by reducing the power of trade unions to resist changes in pay and conditions, removing regulations from business, and privatising industries and assets owned by the state. All of these measures involved not a passive but an active state: a state strong enough to break political resistance to policies that were aimed at removing obstacles to the creation of a dynamic, entrepreneurial economy. This was in keeping with one of the oldest strands in neoliberalism, the ordo-liberalism influential in postwar Germany. The Ordo-Liberals had rejected the old economic liberalism of laissez-faire, arguing that only the state had the power and the authority to create and sustain the conditions for a free market economy. But for Ordo-Liberals that included social policies to ensure that the economic growth which a free market economy created was shared with all citizens and did not merely benefit a wealthy class of owners.

The Anglo-American variants of neoliberalism that became dominant in the 1970s and 1980s, had a different emphasis. They were much more critical of the various forms of the welfare state, which had emerged after 1945, seeing them as major obstacles to reviving economic growth. They still, however, were very optimistic that their policies would work for everyone. Favourite mantras of the neoliberals in the 1980s included the claim that a rising tide would lift all boats, and that cutting taxes on the rich would benefit the poor through the mysterious workings of the Laffer curve and 'trickle down'. Allied to this was the assumption, well grounded in historical experience, that once the fundamentals of the economy had been got right, there would be a guaranteed rise in living standards. The expectation that every American generation would end up better off than the previous one was part of the social contract between government and people.

In the early years of the neoliberal era there was great economic optimism among neoliberals that once the western economies moved decisively in the direction of freer markets, lower taxes and sound money, great energy and dynamism would be unleashed. But political conflict in many countries around neoliberal policies was intense and it took time even in the most neoliberal inclined governments to overcome these. There were also many policy mistakes made, which meant there were a few false starts and economic recovery was often uneven, but in the course of the 1990s a major upswing got under way. Here at last it seemed was the tide to lift all boats. Its causes were many. The end of the Soviet Union and the cold war in 1991 led to a considerable enlargement of the international market order and the possibility of the re-creation of One World, a single international political and economic order. This seemed to be further demonstrated by the emergence of the rising powers, particularly China, India and Brazil. Their exceptional growth rates, and the size of their populations, raised the prospect of a major shift in the balance of the international economy. In the meantime, the flow of cheap goods led to a proliferation of complex production chains in the international economy and downward pressure on prices. In this new wave of expansion, some countries like Germany and China became major exporters, amassing huge trade surpluses, while other countries such as the US and the UK became major importers, expanding their domestic markets and shifting the balance of their economies from manufacturing to services.

The new growth model which emerged particularly in the Anglo-American world was finance-led growth. It rested on what

Colin Crouch has termed privatised Keynesianism. Instead of the expansion of demand being provided by governments, it was provided by the willingness of firms and households to accept much higher levels of debt. This was arranged through a rapidly growing financial services industry. It produced a series of asset bubbles, the most important of which was the housing market bubble. Finance-led growth involved financialisation, the process by which households and individuals become more self-reliant, more autonomous, less dependent on the state, more willing to take on higher levels of debt to navigate the life cycle, and acquire the assets and skills they needed to do so. The counterpart to rising household indebtedness to sustain consumption was ever more flexible labour markets, which encouraged employers to outsource work to countries where labour was cheap, and also to bring in immigrant labour to the domestic economy.

The problem with the finance-led growth model was that it was very successful for a time, but ultimately the very conditions for its success undermined it and precipitated the financial crash. The wave of expansion that was unleashed was most significant in terms of the growth rates achieved by the rising powers, particularly China. In the western economies the growth was substantial but did not match the postwar boom in the 1950s and 1960s. It was also marked by stagnation of living standards for the great majority, particularly after 2000, and by a declining labour share in national income, and a corresponding big increase in the share of property. This was associated with the strong trends towards much greater inequality. The rewards for the top one per cent of income earners were remarkable. The ratio between the pay of chief executives and the pay of the lowest paid employee widened dramatically, sometimes to as much as 400:1. A new class of super-rich emerged. At the same time, the transformation of economies towards services led to a residue of left-behind regions and workers, and workless households dependent on welfare. Governments increasingly resorted to active labour markets to deal with this problem, but with only partial success. Those in work increasingly found it necessary to incur higher personal debt and were subject to a labour market in which increasing numbers of jobs were temporary, insecure and low-paid. In this way, there grew up a sharp disjuncture between the official optimistic message promulgated by self-confident global elites about the success and inevitability of the new global order and the reality for an increasing number of people trapped either in worklessness or low-paid occupations and run-down cities. Many groups did benefit from neoliberalism, particularly those able to get on the property ladder and also acquire other assets, such as pension rights and savings. All these were heavily subsidised by governments, partly to create stable bases of electoral support, and partly to aid the expansion of the financial services industry, which developed new kinds of saving and insurance schemes for every eventuality. One consequence has been that since the crash, the amount of idle savings in the world economy seeking returns which are not available far exceeds the GDP of even the largest economies.

If neoliberalism is understood as a broad institutional and policy framework rather than a specific doctrine or programme, then it is easy to appreciate that all governments since the 1980s have been obliged to be neoliberal since they had to acknowledge the nature of the world in which they operated and the constraints that imposed. At the same time, there was scope for considerable variation within the neoliberal framework. Some governments, like that of New Labour in the UK, used the opportunity that economic growth provided to increase spending on public services by large amounts in the early years of the 21st century. There was a range of possible choices governments could and did make. But so long as a state wished to participate in the increasing flows of goods, services, capital and people in the international economy it had to accept the basic rules of this order, which were neoliberal.

Since the 2008 financial crash, government efforts have been devoted to shoring up a collapsing banking system and trying to recreate the conditions for another burst of neoliberal growth. Social democratic policies have been generally abandoned in favour of austerity programmes, involving cuts in spending on public services because of the overriding need to protect first the banking system and then more generally asset values in the economy which underpin corporate profits and household incomes. The measures adopted averted a major slump, but they could not counter the increasing strength of deflationary tendencies in the economy which were present before the crash, and even greater after it.

Citizens still expected to be taxed as little as possible and to get high returns on their investments and savings. Companies resisted any reregulation of their affairs, and wanted to preserve as flexible labour markets as possible, which meant no change in their ability to outsource production or to recruit immigrant labour. Banks lobbied hard against any suggestion that they should have a license to operate in return for being recognised as too big to fail and accorded government protection. There was still a strong presumption that markets were good and governments bad, and this inhibited any radical thinking about how to return to growth. There was widespread denial about the urgency of tackling climate change and ensuring that any future growth model was both inclusive and sustainable. The growth in inequality was reversed a little in the aftermath of the crisis, mainly because of the fall in asset values, but analysts expected this trend to be reversed as the austerity programmes took effect because the cuts were disproportionately concentrated on the poor and low-paid. Another big spike in inequality in the next few years is expected.

Neoliberalism failed to create a long-term framework for inclusive growth. Many lower-paid workers in the advanced economies did not benefit from the prosperity that was created, and this was because the success of the neoliberal growth model distributed wealth to the top of the income tree in the advanced economies and to middle-income citizens in the rising economies of India and China. By removing many of the institutional factors, like trade unions, which had helped keep up labour's share, and by deregulating the private sector and reconfiguring much of the public sector, conditions were created which distributed the gains from growth very unequally. The contrast with the postwar Keynesian social democratic period is stark. Social democratic governments did make neoliberal growth more inclusive for a time, but they still had to accept the pressures for much greater inequality. Once the boom burst, then most of the inclusive social democratic programmes came under attack, and have been substantially reduced in many countries.

The western economy appears caught in a secular stagnation. It is proving very difficult to raise productivity and investment and living standards, despite the huge pool of idle corporate and personal savings. The response of the new Trump administration is to plan to slash taxes on the rich and on corporations, while reducing spending on services relied on by the poor in the hope that this will kickstart the economy in conjunction with a huge infrastructure programme financed from borrowing, and a more protectionist trade policy. The dream is that, as in the 1980s, a new growth surge can be brought about, and deflation defeated. But conditions are much more difficult today, so this policy is unlikely to succeed, and far from bringing back traditional jobs and raising incomes for the communities that have been left behind, it will increase inequality even further. Neoliberal policies are themselves the barrier to inclusive growth. More radical action will be required, the political conditions for which are yet to emerge.

REPRESENTING NEEDS

A new language for politics and economics

Lawrence Hamilton

Brexit and Trump will be analysed for some time to come, but one thing is already clear. They result from two failures of representation. First, political elites – political representatives, the 'establishment' – have failed to convince that they properly and effectively represent citizens' needs and interests. Second, the strong sentiment that globalisation is the main cause of the ills of advanced capitalist societies is a scapegoat made possible by inadequate representation. I suggest that at least part of the cause of these failures of representation emanates from a certain way of thinking about and judging in politics that has held sway for at least a couple of centuries: utilitarianism (subsequently overlaid with rights-based politics, about which here I say no more, but see Hamilton 2003). The remedy, I submit, is to use the language of needs and interests and what follows from this in terms of understanding political economies: a focus on representation and institutional reform.

Needs are all about us. Humans, animals, corporations, states; they all have them. Though this is not mirrored in the work of most political and economic theorists, a few notable exceptions notwithstanding: Aristotle (1980, 1988), Smith (1975, 1976), Marx (1992, 1973, 1976-8, 1996), Sen (1985a, 1985b, 1987a, 1987b, 1993),

Wiggins (1998). This is especially true of neoclassical economics, for reasons trenchantly defended by Marshall (1964).

Why? The short answer is the triumph of utilitarianism and the justification it provides for a mechanistic view of the polity and the economy, which ends up in the idea that markets can manage themselves, responding organically to preferences via the price mechanism, and the view that individual political preferences are not only sovereign but can successfully be aggregated to generate coherent decision outcomes. In other words, with a few caveats thrown in, the legacy of utilitarianism provides justification for purely preference-based economics and politics (Bentham 1970; Becker and Stigler 1977; Menger 1981; Arrow 1963; Sen 1970, 1973, 1976-7; Sen and Williams 1982).

In the real world of politics, this triumph of utilitarianism within economics has had unfortunate consequences. Utilitarianism's subject-relative approach to morality, which treats pleasure or desire-satisfaction as the sole element in human good, has provided constant support for the reduction of economics and politics to the aggregation of individual preferences (or avowed wants). This involves an understanding of human agency as equivalent to utility maximisation. In other words, utilitarianism offers justification for the evaluation of individual actions or social achievement in terms of their consequences on individual or social utility, as determined by individual preference alone. The concept of preference has therefore come to be prioritised because of its alleged epistemological importance in calculating individual welfare and the moral imperative to respect the judgement of individuals (as expressed in their preferences).

While these matters are of consequentialist reasoning—epistemology and the sovereignty of individual judgement are vital in any form of individual or social evaluation—the utilitarian framework for understanding and safeguarding them is counterproductive. In its quest for a universal 'calculus', it has excluded most of the real world that it purports to understand. Utilitarianism's prioritisation of subjective preferences excludes any systematic understanding of how preferences have, in fact, been formed and any evaluation of how they are and ought to be transformed within, for example, existing state institutions, legal practices, welfare provision, production and consumption practices and so on (Hamilton 2003, pp. 7–8). This is exemplified in the ethical impoverishment of mainstream economics and the demise therein of both the concept of 'human needs' and objective ethical analysis. Worse are the general effects of this mechanistic calculus: a principled allergy against providing a coherent understanding of human agency and political judgement. Utilitarian 'calculus' obviates the need for understanding real judgement about central matters such as individual wellbeing, who to elect and how best to proceed. It also undermines interrogating the processes of representation, for the latter quickly seems superfluous.

By reducing human choice, judgement and wellbeing to self-interested satisfaction of desire, the prevailing utilitarian-informed models and institutions for policy formation depend on a view of the political economic world that artificially reduces human motivation to the single dimension of utility maximisation. Although economics is (or at least ought to be) concerned with real people and their actions, the reductive character of the prevailing discourse is unable to explain many actual motivations for action, most of which directly impact upon economic agency. For, in the market, and elsewhere, while real people are motivated by utility maximising self-interest, they are also driven by self-hate, habit, prudence, ethical principles, ethical ideals, altruism, manipulation, coercion and so on.

By contrast, properly conceived, the idea of human need constitutes a normatively and historically rich tool for understanding most human goods and motivations for actions as well as a practicable mechanism around which to organise policy and think about representation and its associated institutional forms. One of its advantages is that, in understanding and evaluating the institutions and practices that generate needs, it interrogates the sources of demand and avowed wants. Another is that it must also interrogate the institutions and practices through which needs are represented and judged. To see this, it is necessary, first, to grasp the nature of human needs.

Human needs are the necessary conditions and aspirations of human functioning. They have three forms: (i) vital needs, (ii) agency needs and (iii) social needs.

Vital needs are the necessary conditions for minimal human functioning, for example the need for water, shelter, adequate nutrition, mobility and social entertainment. They are 'vital needs' because their satisfaction is a necessary condition for *vita*, or life. This is more obvious with needs such as oxygen and water than for, say, adequate shelter. But the lack of satisfaction of any of these needs tends to impair healthy human functioning (Braybrooke 1987; Doyal and Gough 1991; Hamilton 2003).

Agency needs are the necessary conditions and aspirations for individual and political agency characteristic of normal human functioning. These include freedom, recognition, power and active and creative expression. They are 'agency needs' because they are means and aspirations whose development increases an agent's causal power to carry out intended actions and to satisfy and evaluate needs (Hamilton 2003; cf. Doyal and Gough 1991).

Everyday needs are not normally felt as abstract vital and agency needs, but as particular drives or goals, for example, the desire to drink apple juice or the felt need to work. Manifest in this concrete form, these are what I call social needs, and include a broad spectrum of needs which are either the focus of public policy or are seen to be of private concern. They are brought to light by bald need-claims, for example, the need for an efficient train service; by the content of public provision, for example, the need for basic income support; and by patterns of production and consumption, for example, the need for a car, as elaborated below (Hamilton 2003).

While it is obviously true that needs are not simply strong wants – needs are objective and normative (Wiggins 1998; Thomson 1987), they directly affect human functioning (Hamilton 2003) and "wanting something does not entail needing it, and vice versa" (Frankfurt 1998, p. 30) – the associated sharp analytical distinction between needs and wants belies a more complicated causal reality. First, wants over time can become interpreted as needs. Think of how easily the desire for refrigerators and televisions has become a legitimate need for these commodities. Second, new commodities generate new wants, which affect our ability to satisfy our needs. For example, the car produces both the desire for a car and a need for more motorways. Subsequent economic and political decisions that shift investment from the upkeep of an efficient public transportation system to the construction of more motorways ensure that, for me to be able to satisfy my need for mobility, I need a car.

The three forms of needs underscore something else too. While the normativity and objectivity of needs is important, needs are not simply normative and objective. They are also historical, social and political. Their objectivity is not universal; they are also affected by wants and institutions, and they change as human nature changes. Thus, the normative force of needs is best captured via an analysis of the history of the institutional environment within which social needs were generated.

The language of needs is not an axiomatic alternative to preference-based politics and economics. The *dirigisme* of the Soviet Union exemplifies how devastating this can be on the ground (Fehér, Heller and Markus 1983), as can approaches to 'development' that assume that the determination of 'basic needs' can safely ignore preferences (Hamilton 2003: ch. 1). Needs-based, ideas, policies and institutions would be firmly focused on what best enables judgement in context (Hamilton 2009). Rather than providing universal alternatives to utility, needs provide a subtle, context-sensitive means of involving citizens more actively in the determination and satisfaction of their needs via forms of representation. This historical, institutional focus must therefore be rooted in an account of power and enabled by policies and institutions designed to avoid domination, for it is existing power relations and degrees of domination that determine citizen power.

This is thus a proposal for an inter-subjective and genealogical evaluation of needs and institutions geared towards enhancing representation and overcoming domination. This depends on our power as citizens to identify and overcome what Foucault called 'states of domination'. Power, here, is the socially determined abilities or capacities of agents in relations of power to identify, confront and overcome domination (Foucault 1991, 2002, Lukes 2005, Hamilton 2014b). This ability depends upon the extent to which citizens can determine and satisfy their vital and agency needs. More exactly, this capacity depends upon the prevailing political and economic institutions and the degree to which citizens find themselves in situations of domination. A situation of domination can take various forms. Existing power relations may: a) mislead me in my attempts to identify my needs, via direct coercion, intentional manipulations or fixed, traditional, non-transformed norms and practices, e.g., patriarchy; b) ensure that I do not have the voice to express my needs, e.g. life under a regime that does not grant me the power to do so, such as apartheid South Africa; c) disable meaningful evaluation of needs, e.g. unregulated liberal capitalism, even if the regime in question provides me with the formal means and freedoms (or rights) to make claims, as is the case in the UK (Hamilton 2014b; cf. Pettit 2006; Lovett 2010). The nub then is realistic citizen power, which is often – if not always – mediated by forms of representation.

Political representatives today administer highly complex economies. Not everyone agrees that this is a good thing – Hayek, Thatcher, Reagan – but it remains an ever more embedded and important fact of life, especially in advanced capitalist economies. In every modern polity, therefore, there exists a prudential requirement of sustaining effective means for citizens to judge, criticise and resist constantly and effectively the prevailing principles of their society's political and economic organisation as well as the performance of their political authorities with regard to macroeconomic judgements and policies (Dunn 1990). Moreover, given the complexity and division of labour of modern states, our lives are characterised by membership of a whole variety of overlapping and interdependent groups and various forms of associated representation.[1] In the face

---

1. I can merely assert here that my use of 'group' does not assume that an individual's identity is determined by a single group identity (or that it is essential and unchanging); it rests on the reality that individuals normally are 'members' of various groups determined by class, interest, social perspective, gender, employment and its lack, societal role and so on.

of this reality, apostles of the 'free market' and 'radical democracy' alike retreat to inchoate ideas around organic, revitalising competition and contestation, with little or no room for state power and political representation. I will now propose a view of political representation, and a set of political institutions, that may help us avoid these dead-ends.

Political representation is normally conceived in terms either of 'mandate' or 'independence': political representatives do or ought to respond directly to the expressed opinions and interests of the citizens they represent (Dahl 1989); or, by contrast, they do or ought to act independently of these interests and judge for themselves what is in the best interests of the citizenry and state (Hobbes 1996; Burke 1999). These two main views of representation assume that all relevant needs and interests exist antecedent to the process of representation itself, and in the former case also that legitimate representation must track interests.

There are four main problems with this, although I only elaborate on one here (Hamilton 2014b). Citizens' needs and interests are not pre-existing and fixed waiting to be tracked through representation. Rather, they require identification, articulation, expression, evaluation and representation. Needs and interests have a dualistic nature – they are attached and unattached, subjective and objective – and this lies at the heart of the ambiguities of any form of interest group representation (Pitkin 1967; Hamilton 2003). Moreover, individual and group interests often become present as a result of representation, that is, they are experienced, identified and expressed as a result of the actions and concerns of representatives. This is the case formally and informally: political representatives actively identify and generate new interests; and representation often occurs via identification, where there is no appointment of a representative. In the latter case a representative, such as a leader of cause, brings forward a claim to represent a group, evidence for which is found in their capacity to attract a following; and members of the group feel they have a presence in the actions of the representative by dint of what the representative has in common with them – causes, interests, identities or values.

So, a different approach is needed based on the nature of needs and judgement, which remains realistic about the following four characteristics of representation. First, representation is never simply the copy of some pre-existing external reality. Representation always creates something new: Tolstoy's account of the Napoleonic War does not simply replicate the historical events, it creates a new version of them in the act of representing it. There is, therefore, always a 'gap' between an object and the representation of that object and this holds in politics too. Political representation opens up a gap between the government and the people. Second, the act of representing creates new versions of the people and their interests, and this creative process gives representation its dynamism. Political representation provides citizens with images of themselves, or partisan groupings thereof, upon which to reflect. Third, it follows that representation generates more than one version of 'the people'. This highlights an oft-forgotten central component of politics: political judgement is usually regarding partisan not general or common interests. Finally, none of the versions of the 'the people' on offer to 'the people' ought ever to succeed in closing the gap between the represented and their representatives. Even the attempt to do so is futile and dangerous. It is not the realisation of democracy but an invitation to tyranny because it thwarts any opportunity for the people to reflect on and judge their representatives; and the effect of closing the gap will be to remove the possibility for the portrayal of other competing images, visions and interests of the polity.

Representation understood in these terms enables citizens to avoid or overcome domination. How so? First, political representatives as independent of ordinary citizens are empowered to judge 'for us'. Second, citizens are likewise able to assess the judgements of their representatives, something they do best when their representatives are unambiguously separate from them and their interests. Third, if the unavoidable and necessary 'gap' is 'filled' with the following mechanisms and institutions, these additional representative institutions provide a means through which citizens can affect the judgements of their representatives aimed at keeping states of domination to a minimum.

a) District Assemblies: i) to enable the articulation and evaluation of needs and interests, the substantive outcome of which would then be transferred by the district's counselor to the national assembly for further debate and legislation; ii) to make available to citizens full accounts of all the legislative results emanating from the national assembly; iii) to provide a forum for the presentation of amendments to existing legislation; and iv) to select counselors for the revitalised consiliar system.

b) A Revitalised Consiliar System: i) would rest on the network of district assemblies; ii) each district assembly would select one counselor for a two-year period, who would be responsible for providing counsel to the representatives in the national assembly regarding the local needs and interests of the citizenry and existing institutional configurations and their links to states of domination, that is, what changes are required to better satisfy needs and interests and diminish domination.[2]

c) Updated Tribunate of the Plebs: i) a partisan, separate and independent electoral procedure by means of which the least powerful groups or classes in society would have exclusive rights to elect at least one quarter of representatives for the national assembly, alongside the normal, open party-dominated processes of electing representatives. Membership of this electoral body would be determined either by a net household worth ceiling or associated measures, enabling those with the least economic power in any polity to select representatives who would be empowered to propose and repeal (or veto) legislation (McCormick 2011, Hamilton 2014b).

I also propose a form of constitutional revision based on arguments for the fallibility of reason, and antityranny, that is, that it is necessary to shield present and future generations from the unchecked power of past generations, but this is not necessary in the context of the UK, which is uniquely free of the problems of a formal constitution. Notwithstanding, procedural safeguards are

---

2. For more on district assemblies and an explanation of my adoption of the term and institution of 'counselor' from Ancient Rome (as opposed to the more normal modern English term and institution of 'councillor'), see Hamilton (2009, 2014b).

vital for the sustainability of these institutional recommendations. Procedural priority would need to be secured to satisfy vital needs and to safeguard counselors and institutions from manipulation and corruption.

REFERENCES

Aristotle (1980), *The Nicomachean Ethics*, trans. and intro. D. Ross, Oxford: Oxford University Press.

Aristotle (1988), *The Politics*, ed. S. Everson, Cambridge, UK: Cambridge University Press.

Arrow, K.J. (1963), *Social Choice and Individual Values*, 2nd ed. (1952), New Haven: Yale University Press.

Becker, G.S. and G.J. Stigler. (1977), 'De gustibus non est disputandum', *American Economic Review*, 67 (2): 76–90.

Bentham, J. (1970 [1781]), *Introduction to the Principles of Morals and Legislation*, London: Athlone.

Braybrooke, D. (1987), *Meeting Needs*, Princeton, NJ: Princeton University Press.

Burke, E. (1999), 'Speech to the Electors of Bristol', in *Select Works of Edmund Burke, 4 vols.*, Indianapolis: Liberty Fund.

Dahl, R. (1989), *Democracy and its Critics*, New Haven: Yale University Press.

Doyal, L. and I. Gough (1991), *A Theory of Human Need*, London: Macmillan.

Dunn, J. (1990), 'Liberty as a Substantive Political Value' in *Interpreting Political Responsibility*, Cambridge: Polity, pp. 61-84.

Fehér, F., A. Heller and G. Markus (1983), *The Dictatorship Over Needs*, Oxford: Basil Blackwell.

Foucault, M. (1991), *Discipline and Punish*, New York: Penguin.

Foucault, M. (2002), *Power*, London: Penguin.

Frankfurt, H. (1998), 'Necessity and desire', in: G. Brock (ed.), *Necessary Goods: Our Responsibilities to Meet Others' Needs*, Oxford: Rowman and Littlefield.

Hamilton, L. (2003), *The Political Philosophy of Needs*, Cambridge, UK: Cambridge University Press.

Hamilton, L. (2009), 'Human Needs and Political Judgment', in *New Waves in Political Philosophy* ed. C. Zurn and B. de Bruin, London: Palgrave, pp. 40-62.

Hamilton, L. (2014a), *Are South Africans Free*, London: Bloomsbury.

Hamilton, L. (2014b), *Freedom is Power: Liberty Through Political Representation*. Cambridge: Cambridge University Press.

Hobbes, T. (1996), *Leviathan*, ed. R. Tuck, Cambridge: Cambridge University Press.

Lukes, S. 2005. *Power: A Radical View*, 2nd ed. New York: Palgrave.

Marshall, A. (1964 [1920]), *Principles of Economics*, (8th edn), London: Macmillan.

Marx, K. (1992 [1932]), 'Economic and philosophic manuscripts', in: L. Colletti (ed.), *Karl Marx: Early Writings*, London: Penguin.

Marx, K. (1973 [1939-41]), *Grundrisse*, trans. M. Nicolaus, Harmondsworth: Penguin.

Marx, K. (1967-8 [1867]) *Capital*, 3 vols, intro. by E. Mandel, trans. D. Fernbach, Harmondsworth: Penguin.

Marx, K. (1996 [1890-1]), 'Critique of the Gotha programme', in: T. Carver (ed.), *Marx: Later Political Writings*, Cambridge, UK: Cambridge University Press.

McCormick, J. P. (2011), *Machiavellian Democracy*, Cambridge: Cambridge University Press.

Menger, C. (1981 [1871]), *Principles of Economics*, trans. J. Dingwall and B.F. Hoselitz, New York: New York University Press.

Pitkin, H. (1967), *The Concept of Representation*, Berkeley: University of California Press.

Sen, A.K. (1970), *Collective Choice and Social Welfare*, San Francisco: Holden-Day.

Sen, A.K. (1973), 'Behaviour and the concept of preference', *Economica*, 40 (159): 241-59.

Sen, A.K. (1976-7), 'Rational fools: A critique of the behavioral foundations of economic theory', *Philosophy and Public Affairs*, 6: 317-44.

Sen, A.K. (1985a), 'Well-being, agency and freedom: The Dewey lectures 1984', *The Journal of Philosophy*, 82 (4): 169-221.

Sen, A.K. (1985b), *Commodities and Capabilities*, Amsterdam and Oxford: North-Holland.

Sen, A.K. (1987a [1979]) 'The equality of what', in: S.M. McMurrin (ed.) (1987), *Liberty, Equality and Law*, Cambridge, UK: Cambridge University Press.

Sen, A.K. (1987b), *On Ethics and Economics*, Oxford: Basil Blackwell.

Sen, A.K. (1993), 'Capability and well-being', in M.C. Nussbaum and A.K. Sen, *The Quality of Life*, Oxford: Clarendon Press.

Sen, A.K. and B. Williams (1982), *Utilitarianism and Beyond*, Cambridge: Cambridge University Press.

Smith, A. (1975 [1776]) *An Inquiry into the Nature and Causes of the Wealth of Nations*, 2 vols, reprinted in: R.H. Campbell, A.S. Skinner and W.B. Todd (eds), Oxford: Clarendon Press.

Smith, A. (1976 [1790]) *The Theory of Moral Sentiments*, reprinted in D.D. Raphael and A.A. Mackie (eds), Oxford: Clarendon Press.

Thomson, G. (1987), *Needs*, London and New York, NY: Routledge.

Wiggins, D. (1998), *Needs, Values, Truth*, Oxford: Clarendon.

THE END OF LAISSEZ-FAIRE

Advancing the national economic interest

Patrick Diamond

'The decadent international but individualistic capitalism in the hands of which we found ourselves ... is not a success. It is not intelligent. It is not beautiful. It is not just. It is not virtuous. And it doesn't deliver the goods'.

J.M. Keynes[1]

The title of this contribution is taken from Keynes's famous 1926 publication, *The End of Laissez-Faire*. The pamphlet was a typically powerful attack on the rampant individualism that still prevailed in Britain's economy and society in the aftermath of the first world war, driven by the belief that individual self-interest was sufficient as a motive force. Keynes argued that while capitalism remained the best available system of production, distribution and exchange, there was an increasingly decisive role for government in the economic life of the nation. The state had to do the things that individuals would not do, including long-term capital investment and strategic planning; the 'agenda' as opposed to the 'non-agenda' of government, a distinction derived from Jeremy Bentham. Secondly,

---

1. J.M. Keynes quoted in G. Shuster, *Christianity and Human Relations in Industry*, p. 109, 1951.

the state had to work through autonomous bodies to promote and advance the public interest; these institutions included universities, research institutes, and even public spirited 'joint stock' companies that were not monolithic, centralised bureaucracies, but accountable and responsive to the public good (Keynes remained intensely suspicious of public ownership and state planning). According to Keynes (1926: 288-91):

> The companion task of politics is to devise forms of government within a democracy which shall be capable of accomplishing the agenda ... The important thing for government is not to do things which individuals are doing already, and to do them a little better or a little worse; but to do those things that at present are not done at all.

Keynes was searching for a 'middle way' between free-market laissez-faire and statist Marxian orthodoxies: this "can be seen as an expression of an Aristotelian sense of balance, with both nineteenth-century individualism and twentieth-century communism being viewed as excesses of the virtues" (Skidelsky, 2003: 375). Intellectually, Keynes set out to harmonise, 'the conservative individualism of Locke, Hume, Johnson, and Burke with the socialism and democratic egalitarianism of Rousseau, Paley, Bentham and Godwin' (Keynes, 1926: 274). This chapter defines the intellectual terrain mapped out by Keynes in *The End of Laissez-Faire*; it applies Keynes's insights to the problems afflicting the contemporary British economy while formulating an alternative approach to political economy, augmented by a series of positive policy proposals. The emphasis is not just on restoring economic growth, but recognising, as did Keynes, that economics is merely the 'means' to the 'end' of securing the good life as far as possible for all citizens.

KEYNES AND THE END OF LAISSEZ-FAIRE

Keynes certainly adapted and refined his views during his career as an economist, author and commentator. Prior to 1914, he was instinctively in favour of free markets and willing to defend unfettered capitalist enterprise. Nonetheless, subsequent events and the experience of economic policymaking in the 1920s and 1930s convinced Keynes that in a world of more integrated markets and capital flows, strong countervailing policies must be put in place by governments to guard against escalating inequalities in the income and wealth distribution; at the same time, states had to work together to oversee and regulate the expanding international economy characterised, above all, by heightened capital mobility (Clarke, 2009). The central issue for Keynes was macroeconomic stabilisation, rather than redistribution, but he came to appreciate the importance of a more equal distribution of purchasing power for the resilience of the economy (Skidelsky, 2011). Keynes's biographer, Robert Skidelsky, attests that Labour in 1931 made a fundamental error in failing to properly examine Keyne's arguments for activist remedies and state intervention to counter the great depression. Ramsay Mac-Donald and Philip Snowdon had become the unthinking prisoners of fiscal orthodoxy.

The British centre left today needs to draw on the insights Keynes developed almost a century ago. His central argument was for a policy approach that rejected the view that on the one hand, market forces ought to be sovereign, and on the other, that the state was necessarily the answer to all economic ills, as socialists had long argued. Keynes 'emphatically rejected' socialist doctrines as, "ideological, obsolete, irrelevant, inimical to wealth-creation, and likely to involve gross interference with individual liberty" (Skidelsky, 2003: 371). At the same time, liberals and social democrats needed a clear-sighted critique of the structural failings of 'dysfunctional' British capitalism.

This is an ever more urgent task today. Radical social democracy and social liberalism since the financial crisis of 2008 has been tainted with the accusation that it has merely acquiesced to utopian market liberalism, tethered to an unquestioning belief in the inherent virtue and efficiency of unfettered market forces. Moderate centre-left governments in many countries repeatedly conspired in the deregulation of the financial sector, while allowing public and household sector debt to rise to astronomical levels. Yet liberalism is part of a rich tradition of critique of society and economy which does not slavishly follow the logic of markets or capitalism, as the Liberal governments of Asquith and Lloyd George demonstrated in the early 20th century; it is time that tradition originating in the radicalism of the later works of J. S. Mill and the Victorian 'New' Liberals, T. H. Green, Leonard Hobhouse, and J. A. Hobson was properly rediscovered and revived on the British centre left. What is required is a vigorous development of the 'new' liberalism that emerged at the turn of the 20th century, with its roots in a broader tradition of democratic and social republicanism stretching back to figures such as Hobhouse, Green and Thomas Paine (Freeden, 1978). This is a reminder that liberalism was once a 'rumbustious' popular movement anchored in working-class institutions across civil society: the trade unions, friendly societies, worker's education, and the chapel (Skidelsky, 2003). It is troubling that over the last century, the civic institutions of municipal 'gas and water' socialism and progressivism were allowed to atrophy and decline.

The revival of a popular 'social' liberalism is all the more essential given the manifest failings of contemporary British capitalism. The UK is much further behind its continental European partners than is usually acknowledged by mainstream economic commentators. Simon Tilford of the Centre for Economic Reform (CER) reports that contrary to the received wisdom, the UK has not been an economic success story over the last 20 years: its GDP per head is similar to France, while the living standards of UK citizens relative to the rest of the EU-15 have scarcely improved since the 1990s. Tilford (2016) makes the familiar point that low productivity is the major cause of weak UK economic performance, as a consequence of inadequate infrastructure, low business investment and a poorly developed skills-base. Moreover in the future, "Brexit is set to exacerbate the economy's underlying weaknesses". The fragility of the British economy has meant that historically the UK has been too unequal and too imbalanced, with growth and productivity too low in comparison to its major competitors. The Brexit referendum result demonstrated the extent of disillusionment with the economic status quo, particularly in regions of the UK that are perceived to have lost out from recent waves of globalisation and technological change.

Since 2008, the British left has tried to exploit the financial crisis to proclaim *The End of Laissez-Faire* in economic management, arguing for a fresh approach to industrial policy and greater intervention by the state. But the left has failed politically over the last decade, since fundamentally it is no longer trusted on the economy, partly as a consequence of being in power when the financial crash erupted. Many of the solutions the Labour leadership currently propose are dusted down from the postwar era: the expansion of nationalisation and public ownership originates from the 1930s and 1940s. The call for 'tax and spend' Keynesian demand management is rooted in the 1960s and 1970s (in fact, by the mid-1970s many social democrats recognised that overt demand-side policies were less plausible in an internationalised economy). The Labour party has also flirted with a return to the policies contained in the Alternative Economic Strategy (AES) of the 1970s such as import controls, planning agreements, and collective pay bargaining; the AES did contain some striking proposals, but it assumed a world in which the traditional working class and the labour movement was a powerful agent in society. Similarly, the AES lacked an analysis of global economic pressures and forces. As the Labour party has sought to resurrect old policy remedies from the past, the Conservative party has astutely seized the territory of government interventionism in an effort to rebalance the economy away from structural dependence on finance and the City of London.

The economist Andrew Shonfield argued in the 1960s that because the left in Britain sought to abolish or at least radically restructure British capitalism at some ill-defined point in the future, it lacked effective remedies to deal with Britain's existing industrial problems. The obsession with nationalisation and the refusal to explicitly acknowledge that a mixed economy with a significant private sector was here to stay meant that Labour never developed a radical economic agenda. To fashion a viable political economy from the left that heralds a break with laissez-faire and market utopianism, social democrats must accept that markets and private capital are likely to remain permanent features of advanced western societies. They have to be explicit about the virtues as well as the vices of market forces; and the left has to be clear about where, and in what circumstances, the state should intervene to alter the outcomes created by markets.

To establish a new political economy that avoids the perils of free market laissez-faire or unthinking statism, social democrats and social liberals have to formulate a clear set of economic objectives:

- First, to encourage greater diversity in the structure of the economy between sectors, an appropriate balance between investment and consumption, and between the south-east and London, and the rest of the UK.
- Second, to pursue improvements in the rate of growth to raise the living standards of those on low to middle incomes, while ensuring growth is socially and environmentally sustainable.
- Third, to ensure greater equality of outcomes and a fair distribution of wealth in society. Crucially, greater attention to the distribution of primary incomes and wages will make it less necessary for the state to intervene after the event through increasingly unpopular efforts at fiscal redistribution.
- Fourth, to fashion an inclusive approach to economic development that seeks to ensure all communities and citizens are able to benefit from technological change. As Schumpeter argued, the disruptive process of 'creative destruction' is an inevitable feature of capitalism; the state's task is to build resilience to ensure all can gain and no-one is left behind.
- Finally, the centre-left needs to develop its own conception of the 'good' economy. It has to move beyond the crude calculus of utilitarianism, a belief that wealth and monetary exchange are inherently virtuous. The purpose of economic growth and improved productivity is to enable individuals to enjoy other

pursuits including leisure; to allow those of working age to care for their dependents, whether children or elderly relatives; and above all, to enhance life satisfaction and contentment. One of the most disturbing developments in recent decades is the suggestion that happiness in western economies is declining despite improvements in the rate of economic growth.

It is clear that *The End of Laissez-Faire* does not necessarily mean more intrusive intervention and planning by the state. Keynes, writing in the 1920s and 1930s, was essentially correct: 'economic radicals' needed to focus on developing a variety of small-scale and localised 'experiments' that would over time have the potential to alter the underlying trajectory of the economy. For example, faster regional growth will depend on shifting more government functions, departments and agencies out of London and the south-east as a spur to employment growth and the development of effective supply chains. Public venture capital funds ought to be launched to buy stakes in growth firms; the returns should then be used to support regional investments in physical infrastructure and human capital. Murray (2009: 36) emphasises the importance of 'transitional investment' – digital, transport and energy infrastructure combined with the modernisation of the public sector to promote and encourage innovation across the economy.

Instead of opting for 'old style' nationalisation, 'hybrid' social ownership models ought to be developed to run public infrastructure, avoiding problems created by the 'botched' privatisations of the 1980s and 1990s. Prominent examples of the new ownership models include Transport for London (TFL); Wales Water/Cymru; and the East Coast Mainline before it was reprivatised. Encouraging universities and higher education institutions to merge will create greater critical mass outside the London-Cambridge-Oxford 'triangle'. John Van Rennen and Anna Valero have shown how strong research universities add considerably to regional GDP.[2] Local

---

2. http://www.nber.org/papers/w22501

economic growth strategies are also vital; as Robin Murray (2009:5) notes, what is required is "a programme of more profound structural change, of a radical transformation of structures and institutions that will be the precondition for a new, qualitatively different period of growth".

At the same time, macroeconomic policy clearly has to be rethought in the aftermath of the financial crash of 2008, and the Brexit referendum result in 2016. What is required is a national strategy for economic reconstruction. Importantly, the International Monetary Fund (IMF) has recently underlined the importance of counter-cyclical fiscal policy, given the persistence of anaemic demand in many advanced state economies, despite the IMF's historic attachment to 'neoliberal orthodoxy'. Indeed, when borrowing rates are low by historical standards, there is evidently a major opportunity to engage in the renewal of national infrastructure and physical capital. The British chancellor, Philip Hammond, sought to 'revisit' fiscal policy in the Autumn statement; he recognises that reassuring the markets is not about how much government can borrow per se, but its strategic purpose: capital investment has the potential to expand the productive potential of the economy. The government should rewrite the mandate of the Bank of England from an inflation target to a nominal GDP growth target, so there is a more balanced approach to the acceptable scale of public sector borrowing. The UK also needs to better manage its exchange rate, as the Centre for Progressive Capitalism has recently argued.[3] That will be even more vital as a post-Brexit framework for international trade and the single market emerges in the next few years.

The Harvard economist Dani Rodrik argues, like Keynes, that global capitalism needs to be "saved from itself" through strategic intervention by governments and public authorities. Yet in recent decades, governments have been less effective at mitigating the risks associated with global economic integration and openness to

---

3. http://progressive-capitalism.net/wp-content/uploads/2016/10/Rebalancing-the-UK-economy-final-online-version.pdf

the world economy. A paper published by Rodrik in the late 1990s illustrates the point: at the beginning of the 1990s, Rodrik (1998: 997) found that in countries most exposed to global trade such as Norway, Sweden and Austria, the size of government expenditure was greatest. The explanation: public spending is used to insure citizens against external risks; in the advanced capitalist countries, effectively targeted government expenditure on welfare and social security protects individuals against volatility in employment, incomes and consumption.

From this, we can see how two particular problems have arisen in EU member states since the 2008 financial crisis. First, the union was predicated on a division of labour in which the EU is a force for liberalisation through the single market, while nation states were supposed to protect citizens from external risk through the welfare state; the social dimension of the EU has remained weak. Yet the inability of national governments to perform this function given rising public sector deficits and a growing debt to GDP ratio since the 2008 crash has imperilled the EU as a political project. Moreover, the inability of governments to constrain the impact of global economic integration through 'risk-mitigating' expenditures illustrates the structural divergence between political institutions and market forces. The historical role of liberal social democracy as envisaged by Keynes and Beveridge was to reconcile markets with politics to reduce class conflict and to foster democratic legitimacy: with fewer tools to alter market outcomes, it is little wonder that centre-left parties are increasingly on the back foot. As Rodrik attests:

A crucial difference between the right and the left is that the right thrives on deepening divisions in society – 'us' versus 'them' – while the left, when successful, overcomes these cleavages through reforms that bridge them. Hence the paradox that earlier waves of reforms from the left – Keynesianism, social democracy, the welfare state – both saved capitalism from itself and effectively rendered themselves superfluous. Absent such a response again, the field will be left wide

open for populists and far-right groups, who will lead the world – as
they always have – to deeper division and more frequent conflict.[4]

Indeed, it is difficult to disagree with Keynes (1926: 294) that,
"capitalism, wisely managed, can probably be made more efficient
for attaining economic ends than any alternative system yet in sight,
but that in itself it is in many ways extremely objectionable".

KEYNES AND THE ECONOMICS OF VIRTUE

Beyond stabilising capitalism, social liberals and social democrats
have to think about the broader purpose of economic growth and
productivity. As Keynes emphasised in the early 20th century, economics should remain the 'means' rather than the 'end' of public
policy; according to Robert Skidelsky (2003: 373), "he despised
money-making as a career or vocation" and believed that economic
growth would eventually allow people to return to "the sure and
certain principles of religion and traditional virtue". Many of the
debates that traditionally dominate economics concern technocratic
questions of efficiency, technology, human capital, marginal utility,
productivity, alongside the role and function of the state. Yet the
economic crisis of 2008 was a reminder of the continuing importance of the 'moral economy': a market economy can only function
effectively if there is a broad measure of social trust. Capitalist
production and exchange might be incompatible with human values
and sentiments that we ought to protect, as well as the cohesion and
sustainability of society.

Keynes's voluminous writings also raise the critical question of
what constitutes the 'good' economy. There is little point in replac-
ing a system of free market laissez-faire with an alternative system
that gives even greater primacy to material production, which is why
Keynes remained suspicious of state planning and public ownership.

---

4. https://www.project-syndicate.org/commentary/anti-globalization-backlash
-from-right-by-dani-rodrik-2016-07

The objectives of improved economic performance was not merely to allow greater material consumption and acquisition of wealth (although raising the living standards of those on middle and lower incomes clearly requires higher growth and productivity), but to improve access to leisure, the arts, culture, contentment, and 'the good life' for every citizen, not only the wealthy and privileged few.

REFERENCES

M. Freeden, *The New Liberalism: An Ideology of Social* Reform, Oxford: Oxford University Press, 1978.

J.M. Keynes, *The End of Laissez-Faire*, London: Hogarth Press, 1926.

R. Murray, 'Danger and Opportunity: Crisis and the new social economy', London: National Endowment for Science and the Arts', 2009.

D. Rodrik, 'Why Do More Open Economies Have Bigger Governments', *The Journal of Political Economy*, Volume 106 (5), pp. 997-1032, 1998.

D. Runciman, *The Confidence Trap: A History of Democracy in Crisis from the First World War to the Present*, Princeton University Press, 2013.

R. Skidelsky, *John Maynard Keynes 1883-1946: Economist, Philosopher, Statesman*, London: Penguin, 2003.

S. Tilford, 'Brexit Britain: The Poor Man of Western Europe', Policy Brief, London: Centre for European Reform, 23rd September 2016.

THE MARKET DOESN'T ALWAYS WORK

FIXING THE HOUSING MARKET

Is the act of government building houses enough?

Kate Barker

The UK housing market works pretty well if we are talking chiefly about second-hand homes. It is rather efficient at pricing the characteristics of different areas and types of house at a point in time. Further, the rental market is also quite efficient at pricing, although in both cases there is probably scope to improve the information available, especially around energy efficiency, to the buyer or tenant. But there are two obvious ways in which housing works less well. The first of these is the supply of new homes (which is what this chapter will largely focus on). The second is not about the market, but about the ways in which governments choose to provide subsidised housing – how much of it, to whom, and at what cost. This is not discussed here, except to point out that if the market side of housing works badly, some of the ill effects will be experienced in the subsidised sector – pressures certainly trickle down.

There were around 3,370 housing transactions a day in 2016 – mainly simple market deals. But these take place within a wider housing system subject to considerable public sector intervention, and concern about the failure of new supply to respond to market pressures is increasing. To improve this, it is suggested that government should take two steps:

- The planning system is now working better – but a big missing element is planning on a wider spatial level than local authorities
- The public sector should be even more active in the land market and in the direct commissioning of development

In the subsidised sector, one positive move has already been made, as in the 2016 autumn statement there was a shift back towards government financing of the construction of social rented housing.

WHAT KIND OF HOUSING CRISIS?

Last year saw ever greater use of the term 'housing crisis'. But this is hardly new; remember it is 50 years since *Cathy Come Home* was first televised. What makes commentators assert that recently the housing situation has deteriorated? The housing market is working well for many. The latest edition of the English Housing Survey suggested that in 2015-16 33% of households owned their homes outright – more than the 29% who owned with a mortgage. In addition, as Danny Dorling has pointed out (Dorling, 2014) we generally have more rooms per person in the UK now than ever. (Though very recently this has fallen back a little, and average household size more or less stopped falling in the UK in the 1990s, whereas in other European countries with similar income levels it has continued to decline.)

The perceptions of crisis therefore come from the way in which the housing stock is shared; both in terms of space (rooms or square feet per person) and in terms of wealth. Space per person has tended to fall in social housing and rise in owner-occupied housing. Owner-occupation itself has been falling – having peaked in the UK at 69.3% in 2002 it declined to 63.1% in 2014. The proportion of households who are homeowners has fallen especially sharply among the under 45s. (For those over 45, the home-ownership rate is over 70% in England.) There are rising numbers of under 35s still living with their parents. Over the past decade an additional

60,000 young people have found themselves in this situation each year, although 35,000 of the annual rise is due to higher numbers in further education staying with their parents.

Other signs of stress include rising homelessness – there were 11% more applications for homelessness assistance in England in 2015-16 than in 2010-11. And the number of families in temporary accommodation, which fell during the early 2000s, has been rising again.

The signs of crisis are less clear in the costs of housing, despite what the headlines often say. For those able to raise a deposit, low mortgage rates mean that the proportion of income paid out for the mortgage has not risen, despite higher house prices. For those in rented accommodation, Office for National Statistics (ONS) figures indicate that in Great Britain over the past five years rents on average have risen little in real terms.

Obviously, very large 'buts' temper the above. Both house prices and rents have risen more strongly in London (as well as fast-growing towns such as Cambridge, and in successful city centres). Younger people's wages have fallen back relatively, as set out in the Redfern Review (2016). So for growing numbers on the margins – the homeless, those seeking social housing, young people renting in London, those trying to buy a home without help from their parents, access to adequate housing is poor.

THE HOUSING SUPPLY ISSUE

Proponents of a higher rate of new supply often make two points. (Note: the data cited in the next few paragraphs are for England only.) The first is that, from 1952 to 1980, housing completions were consistently more than 200,000 annually and frequently much higher, peaking at 352,000 in 1968. This included a large share of local authority building (local authorities alone built almost 200,000 in 1954). Since 1984, local authority and housing association new supply, taken together, has never exceeded 35,000 a year. Private housebuilding, which peaked at just over 200,000 in 1968, has also fallen back. Since 1990, the highest annual rate of private completions was 154,000 in 2007. Since the financial crisis, there have been six years of private enterprise completions below 100,000; although 2015 and 2016 saw some improvement.

However, this is misleading to some extent. Postwar, there was a shortage of housing due to bomb damage and much demolition of housing considered no longer fit for purpose. After adjusting for demolitions, the rate of completions was much lower, with only a couple of years above 250,000. It is still true that new supply has fallen back, but the decline is much less dramatic on a net basis, and it is important to remember the public will to tackle the large postwar shortage.

The second point is that England has recently been building at well below the rate needed to keep up with population growth. In 2007, the ONS household projections for the next 20 years were for 233,000 households per year in England. The most usually cited data for household completions, however, increased by just 133,000 per year in the decade to 2015, implying an under-build of 1m dwellings. That sounds like a crisis in itself. But the fuller data published by the Department for Communities and Local Government (DCLG), the 'net additions' series which allows for demolitions, conversions and has a fuller picture of completions, puts the annual rate over the same decade as 166,000. So the undersupply has been smaller, and met in part by more young people living at home and a decrease in vacant stock; the remaining gap is starting to appear at the bottom of the housing chain in the rising figures for the homeless and those in temporary accommodation.

Data has to be handled with care to tell the full story. But it is true that private developers did not increase the rate of supply as much as expected when the public sector cut back during the 1990s, and also that recent years have seen the buildup of problems, especially in hotspots in and around London. Further, we may be reaching the limits of huddling up. If current trends persisted through the next decade, the word 'crisis' would become apposite.

WILL PRIVATE SECTOR SUPPLY DELIVER?

The existence of two sets of supply data makes it harder to comment on recent trends. On the less accurate measure, private sector supply in England has already risen from a low point of 83,000 in 2010 to 115,000 in 2016. A plausible guess is that on the more comprehensive measure, including office conversions, the private sector produced around 140-150,000 units in 2015-16 on a rough estimate. If the housing market remains reasonably stable over the next five years or so (meaning no shock from a sharp economic downturn, nor a marked increase in interest rates), private sector output will probably continue to increase, and could well run at around 170,000 per year. Of this, around half might be expected to come from the 10 largest housebuilders, who work to optimise their position within the present planning system and land market.

Criticism of the large developers is at present largely focused on the supply issue. It is frequently suggested that the major housebuilders should all simply increase their annual output, given that all have quite long landbanks in terms of years of production (the exact length of landbanks is uncertain due to inconsistent reporting across the industry). However, each firm will have some view of its own capacity – in terms of being able to run an efficient organisation and also of its appetite for financial risk. In the major downturn after the financial crisis, the requirement to write down the value of landbanks hit balance sheets hard and ran up against banking covenants for several firms. Since then the value of land has risen, and most large developers have far stronger balance sheets – but do not wish to start using land at a faster rate, requiring longer landbanks and potentially higher borrowing. Further, this would exacerbate concentration in the homebuilding industry – already considered by many to be undesirably high.

Developers need landbanks as these form the raw material required for the businesses to operate. With a core of permanent staff to keep busy and the overheads of a sizeable listed company, it's important to have a clear line of sight to output over at least the next two years, and reasonable predictability for the next two. Planning permissions are often unexpectedly delayed or refused (or even granted more quickly than expected) so the businesses need a range of potential sites.

There is also a view that planning permissions, once granted, are built out too slowly (or even not built out at all). The data here needs careful interpretation, as it is not always clear how accurately lapsed permissions or part-built sites are taken account of. It is worth remembering that it is costly to get permissions for a large site, and that there is already a cost of holding the land empty. This incentive to build a site out is balanced by a desire not to overproduce in any local market. Post the financial crisis, the sharp decline in the number of smaller developers has meant that a greater share of planning permissions are for large sites. In any area, there will only be so many people wanting a new house in that precise location – developers aim to respond to that demand.

It may be unrealistic to expect the present private developers to be the solution on supply, in part due to the sharp decline in the number of SME developers who in the past would have identified and built out small sites. With funding for these firms still difficult, and the planning system perceived as somewhat unpredictable; the result is a supply constraint. This is being filled to some extent by build to rent, often in the shape of blocks of flats using different contractors from the traditional housebuilders.

THE ROLE OF GOVERNMENT AT PRESENT

The public sector plays two distinct roles in housing supply. One is through the planning framework together with the carrots and sticks which push appropriate local authorities towards development, even where it is not popular with local voters. The second is through the use of public land, and through the willingness to be an actor in the land market itself.

Under the coalition government, there were targets for the disposal of public land, set in terms of the number of dwellings this land would accommodate. In June 2015, a National Audit Office (NAO) report concluded that while sufficient land to meet the 100,000 dwellings target had been sold, there was no record of how many homes had been built on the sites, nor of the proceeds from the sales (NAO, 2015). It could be added that it was also uncertain that the new dwellings would all prove additional to what would have been built anyway.

For the present parliament, the target is to dispose of surplus public land with capacity for at least 160,000 homes by 2020. In July 2016, another report (NAO, 2016) pointed out that this programme was off to a slow start. Again, it will be hard to know how many of these sites will prove to be additional, and the focus on 'value for money' can often mean that the public sector, like every other landowner, seeks to maximise receipts to use for other purposes.

A MORE ACTIVE GOVERNMENT ROLE

While the market system works well for many, and the planning framework is much improved, nevertheless new housing supply seems to be stuck at a suboptimal equilibrium. In some respects, little has changed since 2003 when in the interim report of my housing supply review I commented: "Low output in the short run appears to suit many players – local authorities, home owners and arguably the industry" (Barker 2003). To change this, especially in the high demand areas, the public sector must be more proactive. There have been steps in this direction, but too tentative and too slow. Major further change to the planning system is not the solution – since the National Planning Policy Framework was introduced in 2012 this, and further tweaks, have resulted in a better and more workable system. It would of course be even better if all local authorities had their plans in place.

First, government should identify some large sites, preferably next to existing urban areas, which are not wholly included in the existing local plans, and set out to acquire this land at a relatively modest uplift to existing use value. The objective would be to create some large urban extensions, following the line of approach in the recent Wolfson prize-winning essay (Rudlin and Falk, 2014). It is of course much easier said than done. In a world of localism, large towns/cities capable of being developed in this way, and thus already magnets for economic activity, would need to be willing to be active participants. In addition, as the prize essay points out, innovative financing schemes would need to be agreed.

But the gains could be very large. Garden villages (for which there is also a role) have the disadvantages of being too small and often not close enough to large settlements to enable the development of good public transport (for example trams or guided bus routes). The urban extensions would also provide the opportunity to develop secondary town centres and new schools; enhancing choice for the existing population. If well-designed, with good green spaces, surely this would be a saleable proposition? The key will be readiness to raise funding to put infrastructure in early, and not to sell the idea on a list of promises which are not then fulfilled. The experience of the new developments around Cambridge, which have some of the elements of these ambitions, is that they are proving popular places to live.

Second, government needs to get on with direct commissioning. This idea was first proposed in November 2014, and there have been slightly mixed messages about what it is intended to achieve. The basic principle seems to be that government will use its own funding to ensure some large sites (five sites were identified in early 2016) are built out at a faster rate than would have been the case if only private developers were operating. Much of the land will deliberately be used for opportunities for SME developers and custom build, providing a basis for these businesses which could help them to return to speculative development.

To succeed, this policy would need to achieve three things. The first is that these sites really are built out quickly and that the dwellings are sold at a good rate – this would be a test of the proposition that private developers trickle out sales in order to achieve absolutely the best price. The second is that some element of additionality is achieved – so that this fast buildout is not offset by slower build in other sites, or by local plans reducing the number of units required in the future. The third is that the decline in the number of SME builders active in the new dwellings market is at least stemmed, and competition among residential developers stimulated. At the very least, the policy will provide government and its agencies with direct experience of housing market operation. It is disappointing that more urgency on this initiative was not set out in the February 2017 Housing White Paper.

CONCLUSIONS

New housing supply in the past has been more sufficient when government was actively involved in building. But to think this means a return to council housebuilding, looking back at the strong supply in the postwar period, is a partial misreading of the data. There is a case for more social housebuilding – but this rests on unmet need among the poorest in society.

The level of new dwellings supply is very much the product of government regulation. Local authorities undertake the allocation of land for different purposes, and huge variations in land value between different uses create incentives for private behaviour that is not always in the public interest. In addition, the recent large swings in the UK housing market have proved difficult for smaller players to survive, and this has decreased competition and supply. To change this situation, and to unlock new large sites with pre-funding of good infrastructure, only a government-backed mechanism looking at the issue across wider areas than just a single local authority could be effective.

There is a strong case for government intervention to support the market to bring forward large urban extensions, some of which may be built on underutilised public land, to promote new entrants to building and to encourage the resurgence of SME builders. But government should not seek to do everything, everywhere. In many locations the present system works well and developers are adept both at finding sites and at identifying the best value use for them. The proposal here is for intelligent intervention, which is additional and starts at the right spatial scale, supporting the search for a better economic geography across England. It is quite a challenge, and one which the recent Housing White Paper sadly failed to address.

REFERENCES

Kate Barker, *Securing our future housing needs; Review of Housing Supply Interim Report,* HM Treasury, 2003.
Danny Dorling, *All that is solid* (London: Allen Lane, 2014), p. 42.
National Audit Office, *Disposal of public land for new homes,* June 2015.
National Audit Office, *Disposal of public land for new homes: A progress report,* July 2016.
Redfern, *Review into the decline of home ownership* (London: 2016).
David Rudlin and Nicholas Falk, *Uxcester Garden City,* URBED submission for the 2014 Wolfson Economics Prize.

FUNDING THE FUTURE

The importance of equity capital in financing jobs and firms

Jenny Tooth

At UK Business Angels Association, we look after the entrepreneurial finance ecosystem from startup to scale-up. This includes working with over 18,000 angel investors across the UK, mainly operating in syndicates and groups, as well as 13 equity crowd funding platforms, 24 early-stage venture capital funds and a significant number of accelerators and incubators as well as key players in the advisory community.

Small businesses are vital to the UK economy and it is significant to note that over 650,000 new businesses were started in the UK in 2016.[1] There is a strong track record for creating and supporting startups in this country and it is vital that we can nurture companies with the capability to achieve growth and scale as a source of strong employment creation.

WE NEED TO BE AS GOOD AT SUPPORTING SCALE-UPS AS WE ARE AT SUPPORTING STARTUPS

When it comes to access to equity, there is a substantial pool of early-stage risk capital to support startups here in the UK. This capital supply has been supported by the Enterprise Investment Scheme

---

1. Centre for Entrepreneurs, 2016, http://centreforentrepreneurs.org/cfe-releases/2016-breaks-business-formation-records/?mc_cid=cd53b7970a&mc_eid=0804ec0dee

(EIS) and the Seed Enterprise Investment Scheme (SEIS), which offer investors significant tax breaks. These schemes have enabled many more business angels and private investors to put their financial capacity behind startup and early-stage businesses, and have stimulated the rise in equity crowdfunding platforms.

Since the EIS was launched in 1993, nearly 25,000 individual companies have received investment through the scheme and £14bn of funds have been raised. The most recent tax data shows that 3,265 companies raised a total of £1.8bn under the EIS scheme in 2015. This is higher than in any previous year. The number of companies that received investment through the SEIS in 2015 was 2,290, with £175 million of funds raised.

It is notable that the OECD has ranked the UK as third for starting up but only 13th for scaling up businesses.[2] It is, therefore, important to recognise that in order achieve their growth and employment creation potential, many more of these high-potential businesses across the whole of the UK need access to a strong, connected supply of risk capital.

FOCUSING ON THE REGIONS WILL BE KEY

There is a strong disparity in terms of access to early-stage equity capital for businesses across the UK: 65% of EIS and SEIS investment is in companies based in London and the south east. A recent review by the British Business Bank of the availability of equity investment across the UK shows that 64% of all SMEs are in the regions outside London and the south east – so the issue is clear.

At UKBAA we are only too aware of the shortage of visible angel investment across the regions outside London and the south east, with the majority of businesses in the regions needing to come down to London to find the investment they need. We are working to address this through awareness raising and education, as well as

---

2.   OECD report (2014) Chiara Criscuolo, Peter N. Gal and Carlo Menon, The Dynamics of Employment Growth: New Evidence from 18 Countries

by establishing 'angel hubs' around the regions to connect existing and potential investors to information about angel investing and to entrepreneurs seeking investment.

There are also opportunities to stimulate and leverage private investment, including the development of regional co-investment funds; and to raise awareness among existing and potential private investors of opportunities to back small businesses in their regions. The government has established a £100m Angel CoFund (now five years old) to stimulate angel investment, but the number of co-investments made with syndicates from the regions remains limited. So more local co-investment initiatives are needed and there is a role for the financial sector working alongside the LEPs in the regions to support this.

THE IMPACT OF CURRENT POLICY INITIATIVES

The government's support of the new £400m Northern Powerhouse Investment Fund, as well as the £250m Midlands Engine Investment Fund, supported by the British Business Bank, is an important new initiative offering the opportunity to stimulate and leverage capacity among venture capital funds and attract private sector co-investment to support the growth of firms in these areas.

The recent industrial strategy proposals recognise the importance of stimulating further private investment to support key growth clusters and to reinforce our core industrial strengths across the regions. The green paper also identifies the opportunity to introduce new strategies and approaches to ensure access to relevant sources of finance for all businesses.

The prime minister's announcement of the new £2bn Industrial Strategy Challenge Fund to support investment in innovation and priority technological strengths will also be a valuable contribution to building growth and employment across the whole of the UK. This will offer the opportunity to leverage private sector capital alongside these new funds to enable investors to back the UK's great innovators.

IMPROVING COORDINATION ALONG THE FINANCE AND SUPPORT VALUE CHAIN

Despite these important policy initiatives, we have some core ongoing challenges regarding the lack of connectivity across our business finance and growth ecosystem and especially in our regions.

There is much to be achieved by improving opportunities for communication and collaboration between all the equity finance players and business support providers in the regions. This includes angel investors, venture capital and private equity funds, crowdfunders and other alternative finance providers as well as banks and institutions working alongside LEPs, universities, science parks, business growth hubs, the local advisory community and business networks. We have the opportunity to create a common approach to boost business' growth and job creation potential in all of our regions. We especially commend the approach being taken by the Scale-up Institute, working with LEPs and key local players to boost capability to support local scale-up ecosystems.[3]

ENSURING AN EFFECTIVE SUPPLY OF UK RISK CAPITAL FOR SCALING GLOBALLY

A further key challenge is the supply of a connected chain of equity capital for the UK's small businesses across all their growth stages. Currently, high-potential businesses lack access to funds to support their long-term growth. At the moment, there are too few UK venture capital funds with the capability to bring significant sums of capital to enable high-growth businesses to achieve global scale.

This inevitably results in companies running out of money and selling too early, or moving out to the US to find the level of investment they need to complete their high growth ambitions. Recent research done by Atomico[4], the proactive European tech investment

---

3. http://www.scaleupinstitute.org.uk/research-policy/

4. http://www.atomico.com/news/the-future-is-being-invented-in-europe

fund set up by the co-founders of Skype, reveals that UK firms are unable to access the same level of further rounds of finance to support their growth as their US counterparts. The report identified that the US has 14 times more capital than the UK for later rounds of growth and expansion capital.

This lack of long-term capital will result in the best of our high-growth companies seeking investment elsewhere in order to complete their growth ambitions and the UK economy will lose out. Skyscanner was the most recent high-growth unicorn to be snapped up by China's Ctrip; and we saw the earlier acquisition of SwiftKey by Japanese Softbank – both of these had their early nurturing from UK angel and venture capital investors.

THE ROLE OF CORPORATES

The £2bn Business Growth Fund has brought access to significant sums of patient capital for many companies around the regions. But there is more to be done to establish a strong pipeline of connected capital to support growth and employment creation in the UK.

There is a significant opportunity for corporates to take on this role, building specialist funds that not only provide access to capital but also international market access. We are fortunate that some corporates are looking to bring scale-up capital and support to the UK's growth businesses, including Cisco, Jaguar Landrover, Unilever, GSK and the more recent Legal & General backing of the £150m Accelerated Digital Ventures Fund, but more could be done at a policy level to attract and incentivise further corporate-backed scale-up funds.

THE ROLE OF INSTITUTIONAL INVESTORS AND PENSION FUNDS

There is a clear need for the government's industrial strategy and post-Brexit approach to encourage pension funds and institutional investors to back the UK's venture funds at this time. In 2014 only

16 per cent of UK pension funds were allocated to UK equities compared with 56% in 1994.

There are opportunities to extend institutional investor mandates as well as workplace pensions to support investment in the UK's high growth businesses by simplifying regulation and removing barriers. Notably the UK needs to have a strong focus on attracting international institutional investment into our funds. We need to address this lack of institutional capital, at a time when we are breeding such fantastic high-growth potential businesses here in the UK.

BUILDING ON OUR INTERNATIONAL LINKS

A further key opportunity – and one that could potentially be stimulated by Brexit – is to exploit our international links not only for trading but also to attract international investment into our funds. The UK has the opportunity to attract new international investors, both to co-invest in existing funds and to set up new funds, including sector specific investments.

This would offer not only additional firepower to our existing equity supply chain but also access to further markets and supply chain opportunities. We are already attracting some key new funds from China and Saudi Arabia, as well as the £100bn Japan Softbank Fund. However, we need to ensure this is not just focused on tech; and attract more funds willing to integrate with the supply chain to back our key sectors here in the UK.

LINKING IN WITH THE PUBLIC MARKETS

The opportunity to enable businesses here in the UK to raise further risk capital through the public markets and ensure that their growth remains in the UK has also been strongly supported through the actions of the London Stock Exchange.

The LSE has a strong focus on connecting with the risk capital supply chain. There were strong public listings on AIM and the main markets during the past year, many of the businesses having had a range of finance from angel investment and venture capital to bolster their growth prior to listing. This has been supported by recent policy changes to simplify the public listing process and create further awareness of the opportunity to use AIM to build and raise further capital rather than selling too early.

There have been many recent positive developments, but Brexit will bring changes and uncertainties over the coming years. At UKBAA, we have a key role to continue to grow the angel market and enable individuals to back growth-focused businesses. It will be vital that we all work together over this coming period to build a long-term finance and support infrastructure that ensures companies in all parts of the country can access the connected supply of risk capital that they need to move from startup to scale-up success.

IN DEMAND

How can we plug Britain's technical skills gap?

Alastair Reed

Sunderland has a longstanding tradition of being the first part of the UK to declare its election results. So the city knows what it is like to be the centre of attention early-on during election nights. But rarely has the city moved international currency markets as it did on the night of the EU referendum. Of the city's residents, 61% voted to leave the EU, well ahead of the forecasts from most pollsters. The volunteers dashing through the night were pipped to first place on this occasion by local rivals Newcastle. But nonetheless they sent shockwaves around the world.

The city encapsulates much of the story of Brexit. Many residents feel out of touch with a London-centric establishment. Newcastle was the only part of the north east to vote to remain. And of the 50 authorities where the remain vote was strongest, 39 were in London or Scotland. The vote was also partly driven by immigration, but somewhat paradoxically the Brexit vote was mostly higher in places with lower levels of immigration. Sunderland is a city with less than 4% of the population born in another country.

Yet, as important as identity and immigration were, it is hard to ignore the economic drivers of Brexit. Those feeling left behind by the status quo were always going to be more likely to reject it. Sunderland's economy has one of the highest rates of unemployment.

Furthermore, 15 of the 20 'least educated' areas voted to leave the EU. In contrast, the 20 'most educated' areas all voted remain.

Regardless of the precise form of our new relationship with the world, the more fundamental economic issues which have driven discontent will remain. New trade deals will not address stagnating living standards overnight. While the job insecurity arising from more integrated global economies will not subside however much we try to protect certain industries or cut immigration. It may even increase outside of the EU.

The imperative is for a clearer sense of how national policies can enable people to succeed. One of the simplest things national and local governments can do is to enable people to access the good jobs already on offer. Even the local areas with some of the most challenging economic circumstances have pockets of success. In Sunderland, for example, half of local construction businesses say they cannot recruit bricklayers. The area also boasts the most productive car manufacturing plant in Europe, yet Nissan struggles to find enough engineers.

WHAT SKILLS GAP?

The scale of Britain's technical skills gap is not always grasped. Talk of skills shortages is all too often seen as a slight on British workers and the education establishment by business. Or it is dismissed as a niche issue affecting the tech or manufacturing sectors that pales in comparison to the number of low-quality jobs elsewhere in the economy. So above all, it is business that needs to get its act together.

Businesses should invest more in training. But businesses would not function if they had to teach every occupation-specific skill on-the-job. Employers can expect a reasonable level of aptitude and understanding when they recruit, particularly for technical roles requiring skills which are specific to an occupation. These roles include everything from welders and bricklayers to technicians in IT and media production.

Skills shortages for these roles are pervasive across sectors and regions. Research by the Centre for Progressive Capitalism has found that in 2015-16 there were 462,000 mid-level technical job vacancies that were difficult to fill due to a lack of skills, qualifications or experience. As one might expect, the manufacturing sector suffers particularly badly. Around three in four manufacturing job vacancies were difficult to fill. Yet around half of the technical job vacancies in the retail sector were blighted by skills shortages. The sheer size of the retail sector and the shift towards 'big data' in marketing means technical skills are increasingly in demand.

Policies such as raising the national living qage (NLW) can provide marginal increases to the living standards of a broad base of low-paid workers. But linking people up to technical jobs can be transformative. The average pay premium for these technical jobs above the NLW is around £17,300, according to the Centre's analysis of job vacancies. Most are open to those without university education and held by those with so-called 'level three' qualifications. These are the same standard as A-levels but more likely to be vocational courses or apprenticeships.

OUT OF REACH

There are three key reasons why these good technical jobs are out of reach for many local workers. First, the UK has a far higher share of adults with low levels of achievement in core academic subjects. More than a fifth of working age adults have an education below upper secondary level – more than twice the rate of the US. 8.1 million adults in England do not have the numeracy expected of an 11-year-old child leaving primary school. And despite comparatively high levels of investment in education in recent decades we remain far behind other countries. Among 16-24-year-olds, England and Northern Ireland together now rank in the bottom four OECD countries for literacy and numeracy.

Second, the UK has failed to develop an effective system of technical education. Writing in 1851 when London hosted the Great Exhibition of the Works of Industry of All Nations, Charles Babbage argued that Britain's industrial supremacy had disguised the need to develop technical education. One hundred years later, this was exacerbated by the failed attempt to introduce a tripartite system of education of grammar, technical and secondary modern schools. The technical schools catered for barely one in 20 pupils in the late 1950s and never took off. So the vast majority of pupils were taught in secondary moderns, which offered little in the way of either academic or technical education.

Although since then the quality of academic education on offer to all pupils has increased significantly – albeit not enough – the opportunities for technical education have been limited and are of poor quality. Contrast that to a country like Austria where seven in 10 upper secondary pupils opt for technical education or an apprenticeship. The country frequently has one of the lowest rates of youth unemployment in Europe.

The UK's system of technical education has also been blighted by constant reforms to the institutions determining standards. The steady stream of vocational qualifications from just the past 30 years tells its own story: NVQs, GNVQs, AVCEs, Applied A-Levels, Diplomas, Technical Awards, Applied General, Tech Levels and Technical Certificates. In contrast, the academic route has been more stable. This has enabled institutions to develop strong brands, for qualifications to have value in the labour market and for young people, adults and employers to understand the system.

Third, too many people are doing courses that are unlikely to lead to employment in that field or to well-paid jobs. Analysis by the Centre for Progressive Capitalism has found a major mismatch in the types of courses on offer in local economies compared to the job vacancies available. One region had a significant shortfall of vehicle maintenance staff but courses were only providing around a fifth of the demand. It also had seven times as many courses in sports and fitness than the number of job vacancies in this field. Another local economy was training a fifth of the IT engineers and technicians required to fill demand from employers.

This mismatch prevents businesses from expanding. Some have to turn down new orders as they are unable to fulfil them. It has also hit productivity growth. While the share of graduates in the UK is higher than most countries following a jump in the 1990s, this has not fed through to a shift in labour productivity. Germany has lower levels of university graduates but far higher levels of workers with intermediate technical skills. In recent decades it increased its – already large – lead over the UK in labour productivity.

DEVOLUTION NOT REVOLUTION

England's skills system offers 21,000 qualifications, many of which have not been around for long. But within this quagmire are a host of technical qualifications with a strong brand that are valued and understood by employers. Completing some electrical engineering qualifications, for example, add an average of £5,800 to someone's salary after three years. This puts them on par with the top apprenticeships, which have preoccupied ministers in recent years.

The coalition government prioritised simplifying the landscape for vocational qualifications. Funding was withdrawn from thousands of qualifications, as was eligibility for school league tables. But this went only so far. It is the latest skills strategy which offers perhaps the boldest vision. Based on the Sainsbury Review, 15 technical pathways will be introduced by the end of the decade. The hope is this will provide young people with a clear choice to make and then a structured route to progress through.

But one should not ignore the fact that it is yet another reform to the system. It is also taking place alongside the painstaking overhaul of every apprenticeship standard by employer groups. Both reforms need to stand the test of time. The government is also introducing a new Institute for Apprenticeships and Technical Education to oversee standards for apprenticeships and technical education.

This could potentially provide the required stability. However, there does not appear to be anything which will act as a bulwark against ministers who want to scrap it in the future, as happened with its predecessors. This needs to change.

Even with a more stable national skills system, construction businesses in Sunderland may not be able to recruit enough bricklayers. The mismatch between what courses are on offer and where the jobs are has been driven by a Whitehall-led national funding system. Combined with a quasi-market of further education colleges and private providers, this incentivised skills providers to look to Whitehall rather than to local employers. Understandably, many have played things safe by chasing the easiest returns and avoiding making big investments in new courses or facilities. So vast numbers of low-quality courses have been churned out in occupations with little link to local demand from employers.

There are of course world-leading colleges which specialise in certain technical skills. This tends to be where they have built up longstanding partnerships with local employers, often where a major firm has put down roots. Nissan, for example, hosts a skills academy for manufacturing and innovation at its Sunderland plant in partnership with Gateshead College. In general though, further education colleges struggle to meet an almost impossible challenge: both to deliver high-quality technical education as well as basic education for those left behind by the education system. Many private skills providers tend to focus on one of these two roles, and then hone in on the specific aspects they are most effective at. That is one reason why private training providers tend to have higher satisfaction among both students and employers.

The devolution deals signed between the government and some city region administrations offer hope. These will pass far greater control over skills funding to local areas. Part of the deal is that each local areas needs to introduce a metro mayor spanning numerous local authorities. This has proved contentious in many parts of the country. Armed with these new skills budgets, metro mayors could harness labour market intelligence to tailor what is on offer to local needs. They should also use this influence to work with local colleges over time to help them specialise in what they do best.

This is not to argue that local policymakers should be micromanaging in an attempt to have one person doing a course for every vacancy – like some kind of Soviet planning system. Of course, people move between areas. But where there is clear evidence of skills shortages it makes sense to tilt local provision towards those occupations.

WHAT WOULD THIS MEAN FOR SUNDERLAND?

None of these reforms are easy or quick fixes. It requires cross-party consensus around a more stable national system for skills standards and qualifications, as well as local consensus on priorities and the will to reform. With these building blocks in place the system then ultimately relies on the strength of local relationships between colleges, employers and local government. It has taken decades to establish these dynamic relationships in places like Germany.

In Sunderland, these local relationships have been strengthened in recent years by the work of the North East Local Enterprise Partnership and the combined authority, which brings together the seven local authorities. More needs to be done though to understand the specific skills shortages holding back local firms and to assess how the existing base of training providers are meeting this need.

Above all, political consensus is required locally. A few months after the Brexit vote, the north east's council leaders rejected the devolution deal which had been agreed with the government, citing a lack of reassurances over funding post-Brexit. The decision jeopardised the devolution of skills funding.

Let us hope that a solution will be found – not just in the north east, but in local economies around the UK which are confronted by difficult questions over how they operate. Local business and civic leaders need to work together and alongside governments of all colours over the coming decades. People's life chances depend on it.

THE GOVERNANCE GAP

COMPANIES AND THE COMMON GOOD

Harmonising the aims of firms and society

Sharon Bowles

In my role as chair of the Economic and Monetary Affairs Committee of the European parliament, the failures of banking and its culture dragged me into consideration of how things went wrong. The litany of complaints was long, led to questions of whether boards knew what was going on with complex derivatives, whether bonuses and other incentives were perverse, and whether share-linked incentives were right. It continued with consideration over whether boards knew what was going on with money laundering and in the UK with PPI, not forgetting that there has been mis-selling before with endowment mortgages and pensions.

Bank-focused changes were pursued in Britain and Europe: attempting to ensure directors had the appropriate skills, adjusting incentive schemes so as to permit more claw-back of bonuses, paying bonuses in instruments other than shares, ringfencing and a banking standards body to address culture.

Nevertheless, people still wondered why directors and boards were not held more accountable. It was all well and good going after rogue traders, but they were a symptom of the malaise, not the source. The question 'why aren't bankers in jail?' by which was meant those in charge, was often answered with 'there are no grounds', referencing tightly drafted supervisory regulations and high requirements for serious fraud. A rough ride before a parliamentary select committee seemed a gentle sentence.

Then, alongside the anger with banks, austerity measures and national deficits focused attention of both public and governments on the erosion of the tax base and corporates not paying their fair share. Where was the justice for society?

Bankers in jail would not have stopped austerity or the austerity-fuelled wider calls for change, but the fact that, seemingly, there are no ways to hold boards to account for events they cause in the wider economy exposes the limitations of corporate governance, notably shareholder primacy and maximising shareholder value.

Some time ago I used the expression "moral banks need moral lawyers", which caused a small flurry in some quarters. I could just as well have said moral banks need moral accountants. My remark cropped up in the context of how to change banking culture and how to give corporate governance and reputational risk a higher profile within banks. At the time it was before the mega fines, US banking stress tests that include qualitative issues like corporate governance or UK criminal measures for bankers.

My line was, and still is, that the surrounding professions have a big role to play. At times, professional advisers have told me that their only duty is to their client, not to the public good. This has also come to me from internal lawyers. They have said that they have to provide advice that is in the best interests of their client, which in turn is the directors, and bound by the primary responsibility to shareholders. This is a pernicious loop. Large fines for banks, new laws on aggressive tax planning and the true cost of reputational risk has had a sobering effect, but who gets the benefit of big companies is a question that hangs in the air.

On corporate governance, I looked to competition law for my inspiration, which acknowledges well that the rules change when a company reaches a dominant size. Why not borrow that thought and apply it where the size or nature of the business requires the common good to be taken into account? I do not mean get all bound up in market share analysis, just take as given the simple fact that it is necessary to consider the effect of your action on others. That is what happens when you are a dominant company facing break up if you get it wrong. It is front of mind, in the mind of advisers; it always has to be taken into account. When it came to wording for legislation, 'duty of care' was the formulation I proposed.

In essence, I was trying to construct what I have termed a corporate governance buffer, where instead of pushing the bounds of everything in order to gain regulatory and competitive arbitrage, it would be too risky to do that. The role of advisers would cease to be pushing the bounds in the interests of the company's profit ahead of taking account of the effect on others.

The Parliamentary Commission on Banking Reform in the UK used phrases like "electrifying the ring fence" to show their intent that pushing the bounds should be painful and proposed criminal sanctions for those responsible for failure. In the US, the way that suspended litigation hung over banks put them in what I call 'eggshell territory': being in the shadow of suspended actions means you have to be extra careful over what you do.

Of course where things go wrong penalties can come from regulators or tort, but good governance is about the speed bumps, the considerations that stop the accident. It has to be a daily matter just the same as profit. That is what culture means.

So how does my thought that there should be a requirement to take account of the common good stack up with current corporate governance and history?

Section 172 of the Company Law Act 2006 has the heading "Duty to promote the success of the company" and then states:

A director of a company must act in the way he considers, in good faith, would be most likely to promote the success of the company for the benefit of its members as a whole, and in doing so have regard (among other matters) to -

- the likely consequences of any decision in the long term,
- the interests of the company's employees,
- the need to foster the company's business relationships with suppliers, customers and others,

- the impact of the company's operations on the community and the environment,
- the desirability of the company maintaining a reputation for high standards of business conduct, and
- the need to act fairly as between members of the company.

This 'have regards' format was the outcome of the extensive Company Law Review (CLR) that was launched in 1999.

My pet hate in this list is the fact that maintaining a reputation for high standards of business conduct is qualified by 'desirability'. So, not the highest of billings for business conduct, embedded in legislation, although to be fair I think the move from a 'need' to a mere 'desirability' happened after the CLR report.

The first consultation document of the CLR steered the path towards debating 'enlightened shareholder value', noting its roots in common law, versus the 'pluralist' approach more often used in continental Europe. Unsurprisingly in an Anglo-Saxon common law environment, while recognising that boards already took account of various factors through common law, which it was said had become confusing and complex, codifying current practice became a favoured approach rather than putting any other duty on the same level as shareholder value. Codifying would at least clarify for allegedly under-informed public consumption that other factors did weigh in decision-making.

The CLR also pointed out that taking other stakeholders for granted, such as supply chain and employees, was not good risk management. The implication was, at least on some readings, that there it belonged with the setting of risk appetite. Furthermore, giving numerous other stakeholders who might have very different primary interests from the company a legal claim would be very confusing. The much-used example is the need to close down a loss-making factory, in an area of high unemployment, with devastating effect on a local community. Without such a closure the long-term prospects of the whole company might be damaged. Thus, it was pronounced, it was not possible to give everything equal weight and the 'have regard' format was adopted.

So it explicitly placed shareholders first and by codifying the 'have regards' at least with hindsight seems to have ensured nothing else is ever on the same level as shareholders.

Parliament agreed that line having heard more evidence as it examined the white paper from the government. Again the arguments became corralled into the 'primacy' versus 'pluralist' camps, with the pluralist camp losing out because there was no collectively proposed format as to how that should be achieved. Meanwhile, even pluralists agreed that the enhanced shareholder value approach was better than nothing. This 'divide and conquer' approach of an easy incremental change put up against a more diverse idea has featured in more than one consultation.

It is a pity that greater mileage was not made of a dual rather than pluralist approach, which is what the Corporate Social Responsibility Coalition put forward where they suggested a 'duty of care' along the lines of that was encapsulated in existing health and safety legislation. (See paragraph 19 of the House of Commons Trade and Industry Committee report on The White Paper on Modernising Company Law). After all, this is not unprecedented because as well as the health and safety example, taking account of the common good was an underlying premise as the UK travelled through company incorporation to limited liability. Andrew Haldane's speech at the University of Edinburgh Corporate Finance Conference on 22 May 2015 traced that history and includes a wealth of interesting references. The Bank of England, one of the early incorporated bodies, still retains "to promote the public good and benefit of our people" purpose from its establishing charter.

Corporate structures and limited liability have been allowed as a privilege by society, rather than individuals having to face ruin for failure, because it releases a more entrepreneurial spirit that, in today's parlance, creates jobs and growth. This promotion of investment is reflected too in the stated mission of the Financial Reporting Council to promote high quality corporate governance and reporting to foster investment.

Over time, various abuses such as directors using companies as private fiefdoms have been taken into account in legislation around the world in order to safeguard shareholders. The Cadbury review, which followed various scandals where investors had lost money, put focus on to financial reporting and alignment of directors' and shareholders' interests. The 2006 Act puts the spotlight even more firmly onto shareholders, whatever its intention, so that the limited liability and public company privilege is managed only on the company-shareholder axis. That has now been found wanting. The other side of the bargain, that with privilege comes duty, has fallen down. The privilege bargain was one with society not investors; indeed it is the owners, the shareholders, that have been given the privilege of limited liability.

However, the nature of modern shareholding is such that it is proving difficult for stewardship to be everything it should be, let alone for it to honour the privilege bargain. That devolves back to those who truly have the reins, which are the directors.

Returning to the list of 'have regards' in section 172, it is far from clear that these are checked off in any systematic way: some commentary at the time of the Act 'feared' that it might become necessary. What seems clear now is that a non-exhaustive list does not carry much weight set against the primary requirement, and that the direction of travel of who sits on boards is not towards those who might police these criteria and the privilege bargain effectively.

An accusation that was made about some banks and other financial institutions was that there was not enough of the right expertise on boards. This has been tightened up in the senior managers' regime and a more general requirement for all companies is in the UK Corporate Governance Code. Unfortunately, requirements for expertise may also have the effect of reducing the number of available slots on boards for generalists and exacerbating the predominance of the same executive circles and group think. In any event, anyone with a challenging corporate governance mindset may well get sandbagged in the on-boarding educational process about the primary responsibility of directors to shareholders. Advice from lawyers and auditors bears heavily in that direction and given the state of law this is their duty. A reason not to do something new, even not to add some extra transparency, is what might shareholders say. With every company statement scrutinised, what if you get it slightly wrong, what are the liabilities? What if it means you are spending resources on things that do not need to be done?

Reporting and results are all measured in terms of figures and outputs. There are metrics for this. What are the metrics for broader outcomes? Some companies try to address corporate social responsibility through various projects and sponsorships to help development in the community, either locally or more generally. These are welcome efforts and beneficial, but they do not redress the balance when society is left behind and the corporate advance is not shared.

So it comes back to what to do? Best laid plans seem to fail. John Major's government put in place remuneration committees to make sure executives had long-term incentives. They have been populated by people cut from the same cloth – when looking for a new chair of remuneration 'experience' will be a key criterion. Now we have salaries, short-term bonuses and long-term incentives: in other words being paid three times to do your job. Why not give the remuneration committee responsibility for fairness and proportionality of salaries and incentives for all employees. It might work wonders for productivity.

Simple multipliers for measuring executive pay versus the median do not work, as the employed workforce can be whittled down to the highly paid and the rest outsourced. However, it seems to me a good place for worker representation. How about a lot more transparency around remuneration committee discussions instead of soundings to keep the major shareholders happy for the AGM vote when many of them probably have similar arrangements for themselves? Indeed is the consultation with major shareholders treating all members equally in terms of information?

Then it comes to workers on the main board. Why not? The biggest effect of workers on the board may not be how many you have to have to influence the vote, it is the fact of them, even one, being there as a reminder of things about corporate governance that need to make it on to the board agenda. To say there is not anyone appropriate in a global company is obfuscation. It is about the agenda, stupid, to coin a phrase. Corporate governance is all too often focussed only around figures. After the inclusion of the 'have regards' there was some speculation about whether that meant having specific board agenda items. The consensus seems to have been no as the 'have regards' were still the things that, allegedly, inherently came up as appropriate. But something has to come up, regularly.

Of course an alternative to micromanaging board agendas is to increase the penalties, such as was done by the criminal sanctions regime for bankers. However, that is the extreme case of failure.

So I come back to the limited liability privilege, which is not as often presented nowadays a bargain between a company and creditors, but a bargain between a company, its owners (shareholders) and society as a whole. It is the privilege of freedom not to have your entire personal assets at risk, freedom not to be so frightened and wrongly approached, perhaps freedom not to be so thoughtful. It certainly changes the risk appetite. It is about time that bargain with society in return for those freedoms is made clear in the prime responsibilities of directors.

That bargain can be honoured by having a duty to protect the common good ranking alongside the interests of shareholders. No prevarication or maybes. No pretending that means taking over the responsibilities of government. It belongs in the heading and top line of article 172 of the Companies Act 2006: duty to protect the common good. And if it is a choice between company and common good then actually, it is the common good that should prevail.

REINVIGORATING GOVERNANCE

Institutional shareholders should step up to the challenge of holding executives to account

John Plender

There are countless reasons for the current anti-establishment mood of electorates in the United States and Europe. Yet a common theme underlying the victory of Donald Trump in the US presidential election, the British vote to leave the EU and the rise of populist parties across Europe is the discontent felt by the losers from globalisation and new technology. Many less skilled workers feel politically and economically excluded. The challenge for policymakers and business leaders is thus to find a more inclusive form of capitalism. That requires, among other things, a fresh look at corporate governance.

In the corporate governance canon there has long been a chasm between those countries such as the US and UK, where shareholders are supreme, and those like Germany and Japan, where employees have a meaningful say in the way companies operate. In the extreme case of Japan, which has been remarkably free of populist antagonism towards the political elite, despite an ailing economy, the postwar model of capitalism has, in effect, dispensed with capitalists. While the country's corporate giants are nominally responsible to shareholders, they have in reality been run in the interests of managers and workers.

It is clearly neither feasible nor desirable for the UK to import other countries' models of capitalism wholesale without reference to its own governance traditions. Rather, the question is whether and how far to move along the lengthy spectrum between shareholder supremacy and workers' democracy. Theresa May, the British prime minister, has shown a clear interest in adopting a more Germanic form of corporate governance involving employees on boards and a more inclusive capitalism. Yet the difficulty implicit in any such move has been demonstrated by the government's retreat from the prime minister's original proposal for employee directors while she was campaigning for the Conservative leadership. The green paper on corporate governance reform, unveiled at the end of November 2016, offered a very watered down version of industrial democracy. In lieu of employees in the boardroom it proposed stakeholder advisory panels together with the appointment of designated non-executive directors to take responsibility for particular stakeholder interests.[1]

This carries a strong echo of the events that followed the publication in 1977 of the report of the Committee of Inquiry on Industrial Democracy, chaired by Alan Bullock, whose terms of reference were directed at worker representation on company boards. A majority of the committee favoured worker representation, but there was a dissenting minority and a powerful protest against the report by business leaders, who questioned the workability of the report's recommendations, as did a number of class warriors among trade union leaders. The Labour government regarded Bullock's proposal for union appointed worker directors as a vital part of its social contract with the unions. But it was in a minority position in the Commons at the time and dependent on the support of Liberals and Ulster Unionists who were not uniformly in favour of the Bullock scheme. No legislation ensued. It was widely assumed thereafter that any attempt to impose industrial democracy on British boards willy-nilly was a non-starter. A similar scepticism prevails in business today, which

---

1.   Corporate Governance Reform, Department for Business, Energy & Industrial Strategy (November 2016).

helps explain the government's backtracking from May's poorly thought out proposal.

Whatever ultimately emerges in relation to employee participation under the present Conservative administration, there are wider grounds for questioning the thrust of Britain's current system of corporate governance. Contrary to much received wisdom, the system has a notable stakeholder bias. The Company Law Review Steering Group, set up in 1998, on which I sat, proposed a definition of directors' duties that required directors to serve the interests of shareholders primarily; but they were also required to 'have regard' to wider stakeholder interests. This approach, dubbed by the steering group "enlightened shareholder value", was incorporated in the Companies Act 2006. The legislation requires that in promoting the success of the company for the benefit of its members as a whole, a director must have regard to a series of other factors (as listed in the previous chapter).

The difficulty with this definition of directors' duties is that the long-termist stakeholder aspirations it contains are incompatible with the discipline of hostile takeovers and the incentive structures that prevail in British boardrooms and asset management companies. The short-termist culture of the capital markets, which respond punitively to any shortfall of corporate performance against expectations by savaging share prices, also militates against the broader view of directors' duties. When management lives in a capital market pressure cooker the interests of employees, the community, the environment and the rest tend to be sidelined

At the same time soaring boardroom pay has contributed substantially to inequality. That inequality has been exacerbated because the incentive rewards that apply to executive directors and senior executives rely on metrics such as earnings per share and total shareholder return, which can easily be manipulated by management, notably by curbing investment in plant and machinery and in research and development, or by accounting sleight of hand. Chief executives often prefer the company to invest in share buybacks, which have the effect of increasing the earnings per share on which bonuses and incentive scheme awards are based, while doing nothing to improve the operating performance of the company. Buybacks are also potentially destructive of value because chief executives have a personal incentive to pursue them, regardless of whether the company's shares are cheap or expensive. Here, in short, is an acute principal-agent problem, which has malign macroeconomic consequences.

There is now striking evidence in both the US and UK that levels of investment in the unquoted part of the corporate sector are significantly higher than in the quoted area.[2] Survey evidence of finance directors has also found that a majority admit to having manipulated profits in order to meet the market's short-term expectations and thereby boost bonuses and other incentive rewards.[3] It is surely not entirely coincidental that business investment as a percentage of gross domestic product has been on a declining trend in both the UK and US. These flawed incentive structures are also a contributory factor in Britain's poor productivity performance.

A second reason to question the British way of governance relates to the role of the shareholder. In the British system the shareholder-capitalist is seen as the key stakeholder in the system, enjoying the residual right to corporate profits after the claims of labour and all other stakeholders have been met. This view of the limited liability company was moulded by 19th century conditions, where capital was scarce and labour plentiful. It allowed the shareholder-capitalist to exercise the control rights over the corporation, meaning that shareholders could vote at the annual meeting on such matters as the election of directors, while other stakeholders could not.

---

2. See Asker, J., Collard-Wexler, A. and De Loecker J. (2014), "Dynamic Inputs and Resource (Mis)Allocation", *Journal of Political Economy*, vol 122, and Davies, R., Haldane, A., Nielsen, M. and Pezzini, S. (2014), "Measuring the costs of short-termism", *Journal of Financial Stability*, 12 (2014) 16-25.

3. See "The Economic Implications of Corporate Financial Reporting", John R. Graham, Campbell R. Harvey and Shiva Rajgopa (2004), a Duke University and University of Washington study that revealed evidence of widespread earnings manipulation in US business. Its survey of more than 400 senior financial executives showed that 78 per cent would sacrifice economic value to meet a short-run earnings target. Some 55 per cent of the companies surveyed would also delay starting a project to smooth earnings. None of the pressures on CFOs have changed since the survey was done.

The question today is whether it is appropriate for the owners of financial capital, which is abundant in a world of excess savings, to have all the control rights in the company, when the real engine of high growth in the modern economy is human capital. The human capital of highly skilled executives and employees is often firm-specific, because the skills may not be transferrable to other firms. These people are at much greater risk from the bankruptcy of the company than the fund managers or pension beneficiaries whose risks are spread over widely diversified investment portfolios. Yet the pension scheme trustees and fund managers, who often take a narrowly financial, short-term view of performance, nonetheless retain the control rights.

Here, then, is an issue of distributional fairness. And it is note-worthy that in businesses where human capital is the driver of per-formance, executives do not hesitate to demand what others regard as excessive pay, partly because they sense inequity in their rela-tionship with shareholders. Hi-tech companies and social networks tend not to need new capital on flotation. They go public chiefly to provide an exit for venture capitalists. The founding entrepreneurs frequently insist on two-tier capital structures so that they can retain voting control while holding only a minority of the equity in the company. They are thus unaccountable to outside shareholders.[4]

How should these deficiencies in the British corporate governance model be addressed? How can the stakeholder spirit of the Compa-nies Act definition of directors' duties be recaptured? On the issue of inclusion it seems to me that – with the notable exception of board-room pay – better answers are to be found in tax, regional and indus-trial policy than in corporate governance. That said, there is a case for having employees on subcommittees of the board, most notably the remuneration committee. This has been pioneered, among FTSE 100 companies, by First Group. But as with the broader issue of workers on boards, it is not something that could readily be imposed

---

4. For a wider discussion, see my "Going Off The Rails: Global Capital And The Crisis Of Legitimacy", Wiley (2003).

by law. There may also be room for experimentation with advisory committees on which stakeholders are represented, as suggested by the green paper referred to earlier, though there is an obvious risk that these could become ineffectual talk shops.

With corporate governance more directly, there is a compelling case for restraining hostile takeovers and for wider curbs on mergers and acquisitions. If that sounds draconian it is important to recall the damage that takeovers have caused to British industry and finance. Imperial Chemical Industries and Marconi, in their time the two biggest manufacturing companies in Britain, were destroyed by making ill-judged and poorly financed acquisitions. So, too, subsequently, with RBS and HBOS, in banking.

In theory the so-called market for corporate control is a way of ensuring that more efficient managers are put in charge of underperforming companies. Yet it needs to be recognised that this is not a market in which thousands of purchasers and sellers participate in a process of price discovery. It is a market where transactions are lumpy and sporadic and where agency problems distort economic outcomes. Hostile bidders are often stuck in a strategic cul-de-sac and may seek to acquire well run companies to escape from the consequences of their own poor management, as was arguably the case with Kraft's acquisition of Cadbury. Or they may be in the hands of managers who are chasing size, which often provides the excuse for higher executive pay. Or, again, managers are often gripped by the thrill of the takeover chase, which they find more exciting than generating incremental improvements in operating performance.

Given the rise of shareholder activists and of more active stewardship investing by big institutions, it could be argued that the need for hostile takeover discipline has lessened. It would certainly be possible to allow companies to deploy so-called poison pills against predators, as in the US where, for example, management of a target company can offer shares at a discount to existing shareholders, so making it prohibitively expensive for the bidding company to complete the acquisition. Yet these remedies have the disadvantage of feather-bedding incumbent management. A better approach would be to impose higher hurdles in votes on hostile acquisitions. For example, a failure to persuade 80 per cent of the shareholders in the target company could cause a bid automatically to lapse. (Kraft initially managed to win the support of only 71 per cent of shareholders in Cadbury for its hostile offer.) Yet raising the bar in this way would still leave open the possibility that a really persuasive case could prevail against a truly egregious management team.

Agreed takeovers of the kind that devastated ICI, Marconi, RBS and HBOS are a more difficult proposition. Once again there is a case for higher hurdles, this time for winning shareholder approval for the bidding company to go ahead with a takeover. Yet with RBS's disastrous acquisition of part of ABN-Amro more than 90 per cent of the RBS shareholders voted in favour of the bid, even though ABN-Amro has sold off what the RBS management had regarded as its most attractive business and despite the fact that markets in 2007 were already in the grip of the credit crunch that heralded the great financial crisis. As with the wider stewardship agenda there is an important question about the competence of institutional investors to make big strategic decisions. It is hard to see how the problem can be addressed except by company boards and institutional investors raising their game. Yet it is not easy to be optimistic on that score.

Much the same is true of excessive resort to share buybacks. Institutional investors should be bringing more pressure to bear to restrain such financial engineering. Policy should therefore aim to make it easier for them to do so. An important means for this is to address the conflict of interest in management's position through disclosure. Companies should be obliged to disclose the positive or negative return on buyback transactions in the light of market movements. Revealing in financial statements the loss on the fall in the price of expensively bought shares would provide ammunition for shareholders to put a brake on such activity.

Boardroom pay is the area that provides overwhelming evidence of a corporate governance vacuum. While institutional investors have become more active in protesting against the more egregious awards and the 2013 Enterprise and Regulatory Reform Act introduced a number of changes to the executive pay setting process there is still little evidence of any connection between pay and performance. And the pay of FTSE 100 chief executives has been turbo charged. In the 18 years to 2015 it quadrupled, largely thanks to annual bonuses and equity-related long-term pay incentives.[5] Yet the government green paper's recommendations on boardroom pay amounted to no more than anodyne tinkering. What is needed is a wider recognition that equity related incentive schemes are fundamentally flawed both in their underlying logic and their faulty methodology.

The thinking behind the growth of such equity based pay rests on the theory that the interests of executives should be aligned with those of shareholders.[6] Yet alignment is a chimera. Chief executives' motivation and risk appetite vary according to, inter alia, their age and personal balance sheets. Even if those balance sheets were the same, with no variation in levels of borrowing, we should ask whose interests those of the chief executives are being aligned with anyway. Pension funds, mutual funds, insurers, sovereign wealth funds, high frequency traders and hedge funds vary greatly both within and between each category in terms of objectives, time horizons and perceptions of risk. The notion of any possibility of alignment is thus a nonsense.

As for methodologies, the performance metrics in long term incentive schemes – which are, incidentally, mostly short term – are fundamentally flawed. They do not and cannot capture the complexities of modern corporate performance or the positive or negative contribution to performance of individual executives. As mentioned earlier in relation to share buybacks, the most widely used metrics – earnings per share and total shareholder return – are easily manipulated. Meanwhile, Andrew Haldane, chief economist of the Bank of England, has pointed out that paying in equity may even increase the probability of failure. Among US bank chief executives before

---

5. Manifest Pay and Performance Survey (2015).
6. The theory was first advanced in Jensen, M. C. and Meckling, W. H. (1976), "Theory of the Firm: Managerial Behavior, Agency Costs and Ownership Structure", *Journal of Financial Economics*, vol 3, pages 305-60.

the financial crisis the five top equity stakes were held by Dick Fuld of Lehman Brothers, Jimmy Cayne of Bear Stearns, Stan O'Neal of Merrill Lynch, John Mack of Morgan Stanley and Angelo Mozilo of Countrywide. All bar Morgan Stanley were basket cases in 2008. This suggests that the reforms which focus on extending time horizons of incentive plans or clawing back bonuses in the event of underperformance, however desirable in the current pay context, are not addressing the fundamental problem. The chief priority in the reform of boardroom incentives should rather be to shrink the proportion of performance-related pay in the total pay package as far as possible. Institutional shareholders thus need to express more forcefully their dissatisfaction with pay plans heavily biased towards equity awards and call for a return to executive pay that is granted substantially in old fashioned cash. In the area of corporate governance this is the single most important means available towards creating a more inclusive form of capitalism.

THE PENSIONS PROBLEM

Time to face uncomfortable truths and make different choices?

Dina Medland

As we head towards 2020, it is beginning to look very much as if the concept of 'defined benefit' in pensions is dead. Growing evidence suggests that such pensions may simply not be sustainable. Or is it a case of rethinking the priorities for corporate cash? Either way, or more likely somewhere in between – but still, no one seems to want to call it as a decision that needs making.

In the wake of Britain's vote to leave the European Union via the June 2016 referendum, there has been even less appetite among politicians and business to confront, explain, and wrestle with solutions for uncomfortable truths. This makes pensions a ticking time bomb at the very time when the government has been consulting to find ways to improve corporate governance and renew trust in business.

Defined benefit has the security that it is human nature to crave. Here is the definition of 'defined benefit' according to the UK government's Money Advice Service[1]:

Defined benefit pensions pay out a secure income for life which increases each year. You may have one if you've worked for a large employer or in the public sector. Your employer contributes to the scheme and is responsible for ensuring there's enough money at the

---

1. https://www.moneyadviceservice.org.uk/en/articles/defined-benefit-schemes

time you retire to pay your pension income. You can contribute to the scheme too.

They usually continue to pay a pension to your spouse, civil partner or dependants when you die. Pensions account for 20% of total UK government spending. In the fiscal year ending in 2016, total UK public spending, including central government and local authorities, was £761.9bn.

Total UK public spending is expected to be £784.1bn[2] in the fiscal year ending in 2017. Of that amount, pensions will be £156.9bn. This compares to £142.7bn for healthcare, £85.2bn for education, £45.6bn for defence and £113.1bn for welfare.

It seems fair to say that pensions are an important financial statement from business about its commitment to its people.

But let's not forget the UK national deficit[3]. For the fiscal year ending in March 2017, the "current budget deficit" is estimated to be £19.1bn. This is as defined by the Office of Budget Responsibility as current expenditure – current receipts – depreciation. The difference between spending (including capital expenditure) and revenue is estimated to be £67.6bn. The increase in UK "net debt" is estimated to be £47.8 bn.

This is a snapshot of some of the numbers that might keep politicians up at night, but being of vastly complicated and unpopular hue, do not make it to the top of the agenda of anyone who wants to be re-elected.

But recent research has cast a new light on the numbers, and at the same time raised critical questions around the role of business in society. According to analysis of FTSE100 2015-16 annual reports by the pension consultancy JLT Employee Benefits, nearly half of all FTSE100 companies could have cleared their pension deficits with payment of one year's dividends.[4]

In examining the latest annual accounts for FTSE100 companies, the consultancy found that the UK's leading listed businesses paid

2. http://www.ukpublicspending.co.uk/government_expenditure.html
3. http://www.ukpublicspending.co.uk/uk_national_deficit_analysis
4. https://www.jltemployeebenefits.com/our-insights/publications/ftse-reports/dec-2016-ftse-100-and-their-pension-disclosures

£68.5bn to shareholders, more than five times the £13.2bn they made in pension contributions.

Dividend payments, it says, rose from £67bn, as pension deficits (as disclosed on company balance sheets) hit £25bn. Only six FTSE100 companies paid more in contributions to their defined benefit pension schemes than in dividends to their shareholders, according to the research. It is based on accounts published up to June 30, 2016. In a 2017 statement, JLT Employee Benefits said:

> There are a significant number of FTSE100 companies where the pension scheme represents a material risk to the business. Eight FTSE100 companies have total disclosed pension liabilities greater than their equity market value. For International Airlines Group, the total disclosed pension liability is more than triple its equity market value. For BAE Systems, Royal Bank of Scotland and Sainsbury, the total disclosed pension liabilities are almost double their equity market value.

This clear inability to choose to fund defined benefit pensions according to the current parameters of best business and corporate governance thinking is mirrored in the global corporate world.

MSCI[5] – whose indices and analytical information help investors build and manage portfolios – recently published a report on concerns around the under-funding of global pensions. It did so under the auspices of a brief around Environmental, Social and Governance (ESG) issues, which have been steadily gaining traction with institutional investors.

As I wrote last November on the Forbes online platform[6], its results are startling. The ratio of corporate under-funding is worst in North America, followed by Europe.

According to MSCI at the time, Britain's BT had a whopping 36% gap between its pension obligations and the resources set aside to fund them. It was then second behind America's DuPont, which had an even

---

5. https://www.msci.com/
6. http://www.forbes.com/sites/dinamedland/2016/11/27/its-about-my-pension-stupid-pensions-are-a-corporate-governance-issue/#32af86d714f4

larger 42% funding gap. BT had around £50bn of underlying pension liabilities, the largest of any UK company, at the time of the report. And yet there continues to be significant funding of pension deficits. Last year saw total deficit funding of £6.3bn, up from £6.1bn the previous year, says still more recent research in January 2017 from JLT.

BT suddenly chose to lead the way with a deficit contribution of £0.8bn (net of ongoing costs), and 49 other FTSE100 companies also reported significant deficit funding contributions in their most

MSCI ACWI Companies with Highest Underfunding Ratio*

Company Name	Country	Underfunded Pension Liability/Revenue
E I DU PONT DE NEMOURS AND CO	UNITED STATES	42%
BT GROUP PLC	GREAT BRITAIN	36%
HESS CORP.	UNITED STATES	36%
DUN & BRADSTREET CORP	UNITED STATES	34%
DELTA AIR LINES, INC.	UNITED STATES	34%
BANK OF KYOTO LTD	JAPAN	33%
CENTURYLINK INC	UNITED STATES	31%
BAE SYSTEMS PLC	GREAT BRITAIN	30%
ELECTRICITE DE FRANCE SA	FRANCE	30%
ENTERGY CORPORATION	UNITED STATES	30%
RAYTHEON COMPANY	UNITED STATES	29%
EVONIK INDUSTRIES AG	GERMANY	29%
MOTOROLA SOLUTIONS INC	UNITED STATES	28%
SOLVAY SA	BELGIUM	27%
FIRSTENERGY CORP.	UNITED STATES	27%
LOCKHEED MARTIN CORPORATION	UNITED STATES	26%
BAYER AKTIENGESELLSCHAFT	GERMANY	26%
CAIXABANK SA	SPAIN	26%
CONSOLIDATED EDISON, INC.	UNITED STATES	26%
HARRIS CORPORATION	UNITED STATES	26%
SWISSCOM AG	SWITZERLAND	26%
NORTHROP GRUMMAN CORPORATION	UNITED STATES	25%
BOEING CO	UNITED STATES	25%
WEST JAPAN RAILWAY COMPANY	JAPAN	25%
ALCOA INC	UNITED STATES	24%

* Underfunded Pension Liabilities/Revenue

Figure 1   *Source: MSCI*

recent annual report and accounts, it said. They appear to have ensured they were fairly quiet about it.

But on the earlier MSCI marker, London-listed BAE Systems remains among the top 10 worst-funded company pension schemes. JLT research found that for BAE Systems, Royal Bank of Scotland and Sainsbury's, the total disclosed pension liabilities are almost double their equity market value.

MSCI examined the pension funding status of nearly 5,300 companies that disclose defined benefits pension funds across four developed market regions – North America, western Europe, Asia-Pacific and Japan. Europe's under-funded ratio comes out at 4.7%, just behind the worst geographical region for under-funding: North America at 9.2. Japan is at 3.7% and Asia is at only 1.8%.

"With a few country-level exceptions, the under-funding ratio increased across all four regions between 2015 and 2016", said the MSCI report.

What made MSCI look at the under-finding of pensions? It was sparked by the very human disaster that has surrounded the corporate demise of BHS[7], the retailer formerly owned by Philip Green which collapsed with 11,000 jobs lost, in one of Britain's biggest corporate failures.

While BHS was hitting the headlines, Howard Sherman, the business manager for corporate governance and accounting at MSCI was watching closely. "As an American working in London I looked at the BHS collapse and thought – how could this happen?" he told me – as recorded at the time in my independent blog Board Talk[8] – when discussing the MSCI report.

MSCI engages regularly with institutional investors around stewardship, so it was an obvious choice of subject for its research. BHS opened the door to a whole new discussion on pensions. As the UK parliamentary report said, it "begs much wider questions

---

7. http://www.forbes.com/sites/dinamedland/2016/07/25/bhs-a-story-of-personal-greed-and-the-unacceptable-face-of-capitalism/#7f3b9ca729f0
8. http://www.dinamedland.com/apps/blog/show/44308334-corpgov-booming-business-and-for-some-pandora-s-box

about the gaps in company law and pension regulation that must be addressed."

It is a question that goes to the heart of a company's responsibilities to its stakeholders, and also of the structural ability of the system to anticipate long-term pitfalls in M&A.

The UK government's green paper on corporate governance reform[9], issued in November 2016, looks to broaden scrutiny to private companies. It says:

> Good governance is about more than the relationship between the owners and the managers of a business. There are other stakeholders with a strong interest in whether a business is well run, including employees, customers, supply chains and pension fund beneficiaries. They all suffer when a private company fails as the recent failure of BHS has demonstrated.

It points out that, since 1999, there has been a steady decline in the number of public companies while in the same period there has been an increase in privately held businesses:

"Society has a legitimate expectation that companies will be run responsibly in return for the privilege of limited liability, a privilege that is enjoyed by all companies and LLPs, irrespective of their size and status" says the green paper, giving further context that high standards of corporate governance "can help provide the necessary assurance that limited liability will not be abused."

But those high standards of corporate governance presumably exist at the listed businesses that appear to be ignoring the issue. At time of writing some of these businesses when approached by the media on the subject have refused to comment on the state of their pension under-funding.

Is there a gap appearing between what are termed the "legitimate expectations of society" and our listed businesses? Or is it also about redefining, with urgency, what those "legitimate expectations"

---

9.   https://www.gov.uk/government/uploads/system/uploads/attachment_data/file/573438/beis-16-56-corporate-governance-reform-green-paper-final.pdf

amount to against a realistic recognition of demographic and economic realities.

MSCI and JLT are not alone to have pointed a finger at the underfunding of pensions. In September 2016, research by Mercer, the consultancy, showed that the annual accounting cost of building up new defined benefit (DB) pensions for the UK's largest 350 listed companies had increased by over £2bn since the start of the year.

The consultancy's analysis of FTSE350 financial statements shows that their service cost for new DB benefits earned in 2015 was approximately £7.5bn ($9.7bn) and would increase to £10.8bn ($14bn) in 2017 for the same benefit accrual.

It said this had been driven by record lows in high-quality corporate bond yields, which are used to measure the pension costs reported in company accounts. The lower the interest rate yield used, all else being equal, the bigger the reported pension cost. It was also clearly one of the many unintended consequences of the Brexit vote. The EU referendum and the Bank of England's expansion of quantitative easing in August 2016 contributed to the low bond yields, said Mercer.

"Our analysis of current low bond yields shows that new DB pension savings now typically have an accounting cost about four times higher than the cost of defined contribution (DC) retirement savings. The impact of over £2bn on profits is material compared with pretax profits of FTSE350 companies of £84bn in 2015," said Warren Singer, Mercer's UK head of Pension Accounting.

In another survey of 167 European pension plans published in November 2016 two thirds said they expected worsening pension deficits against a rising tide of nationalism and political and economic uncertainty. The number of UK pension plans in deficit increased to 4,995 after the Brexit vote, revealed the report[10] by asset management firm Amundi and the consultancy Create.

Government guarantees on pensions have been cited as one reason not to be overly concerned about this trend. But according to a

---

10. http://research-center.amundi.com/page/Videos/2016/2016-11/Expecting-the-unexpected-our-latest-report-for-Pension-providers?search=true

report by the Pensions Institute[11] at London's Cass Business School, a worst-case scenario could see 1,000 more pension funds enter the PPF.

Despite all the talk about the importance of looking at the longer term and rethinking the role of business in society, it seems there is still a tendency to look at the implications of ballooning pension deficits only in terms of the threat of a potential halt in dividend payments.

If one of the aims of corporate governance reforms is to re-establish and maintain public trust in business, any potential threat to corporate sustainability via a major impact to stakeholders surely comes high on the agenda.

A recent poll by ICSA: The Governance Institute of company secretaries in Britain's boardrooms found that almost two thirds of those surveyed felt that The Pensions Regulator (TPR) should be given stronger powers to block takeovers in order to safeguard pensions. Some 55% of those surveyed also felt that directors' duties should be expanded to include a specific 'duty of care' for a company's pension fund.

Allocating boardroom responsibilities provides recognition there is a problem, but it does not resolve the underlying issue. If defined benefit is dead, it is because it is no longer affordable in its existing form – given the commitment to short-term dividend pay outs to shareholders.

The UK government's recent legislative changes to pensions[12] and automatic enrolment[13] are a major step forward. More than 6.7m workers have since been placed in workplace pensions by more than 250,000 employers, and it is now examining how to draw millions of self-employed workers into saving for a pension.

---

11.   http://www.pensions-institute.org/reports/GreatestGood.pdf
12.   https://www.autoenrolment.co.uk/knowledge-bank/in-depth-articles/pension-changes
13.   http://www.pensionsadvisoryservice.org.uk/about-pensions/pensions-basics/automatic-enrolment

But by August 2016, the total funding gap of British pensions hit a record high of £945bn[14] according to Hymans Robertson, the consultancy.

In November 2016, seven local councils in the West Midlands said "unrelenting" cuts to their budgets had left them unable to bail out the £11.5bn West Midlands Pension Fund (WMPF), the region's largest public sector pension scheme. It is one of 89 funds in England's Local Government Pension Scheme[15], which has five million members.

But the LGPS was described back in 2015 as "unsustainable" by the Centre for Policy Studies[16] thinktank, due to past underfunding and because retirees are living longer.

Looking at Europe as a whole, the pension savings gap is now 13% of the European Union's 2016 GDP, according to the results of Aviva's second 'Mind the Gap' report[17] in September 2016.

"At an eye-watering €2tn, Europe's annual pension savings gap is significant, growing and is now one of the most pressing long-term policy issues facing governments and individuals across the region" said David McMillan, Chief Executive Officer, Aviva Europe.

He went on to add:

No single policy measure will close the gap alone, urgent action is required on four different fronts – building pension systems that offer stability, increasing access to pensions, better pension information, and helping individuals take informed decisions. Governments, companies and individuals can work together to bridge the gap, but there is no time for delay if we want future generations to have a secure and prosperous retirement.

---

14.   https://www.financialdirector.co.uk/2016/08/09/pension-scheme-funding-gap-widens-further-on-boe-rate-cut/
15.   https://www.gov.uk/government/uploads/system/uploads/attachment_data/file/562581/LGPS_England_2015-16.pdf
16.   http://www.cps.org.uk/publications/reports/the-local-government-pension-scheme-crisis-awaits/
17.   http://www.aviva.co.uk/media-centre/story/17667/european-pension-savings-gap-reaches-2-trillion-a-/

Both the collaborative nature of action needed and the emphasis on better information and individual decision-taking resonates in his words.

They were also critically present in a speech given by Andrew Bailey[18], chief executive at the UK regulator the Financial Conduct Authority (FCA), delivered at the 24th Pensions and Savings Symposium at Gleneagles in Scotland last September.

Pensions and long-term retirement savings are probably top of the list in terms of their importance to our society, he said. In conclusion, he went on:

Retirement saving and pensions is one of the largest issues we face. It needs to be considered broadly. There are some very big issues at stake here: the balance of who takes the risk, between the state, employers and individuals, with the balance shifting to individuals; the potential for large inter-generational shifts in income and wealth; the impact of heightened macroeconomic uncertainty on the ability to write long-term financial contracts which embed assumptions on future returns ... and finally, the big issue of the appropriate balance of public policy between positive descriptions of the issue – retirement savings and pension provision – and more normative prescription from public authorities to individuals. These are the big issues.

They are big issues that need to be tackled openly, as part of a duty of care, before they cause societal discord due to sheer lack of individual knowledge and understanding.

Business needs to be a critical part of that open conversation about what it does with excess corporate cash.

---

18.   https://www.fca.org.uk/news/speeches/pensions-and-long-term-retirement-saving-macroeconomic-perspective